# ON HEROISM

## McCain, Milley, Mattis,
## and the Cowardice of Donald Trump

JEFFREY GOLDBERG

**zando**
NEW YORK

Zando
zandoprojects.com

First Edition: September 2024

Text and cover design by Oliver Munday

The publisher does not have control over and is not responsible for author or other third-party websites (or their content).

Library of Congress Control Number: 2024935415

978-1-63893-204-8 (Paperback)
978-1-63893-205-5 (ebook)

10 9 8 7 6 5 4 3 2 1
Manufactured in the United States of America

# CONTENTS

*For Pamela*

# INTRODUCTION

HERE IS A STORY ABOUT honor, told to me by the habitually dishonorable Henry Kissinger. The scene: negotiations between the U.S. and North Vietnam that eventually led to the Paris Peace Accords. I heard this story from Kissinger during the 2008 presidential campaign, in an interview whose main subject was the record and character of the Republican nominee, John McCain, the Arizona senator and former prisoner of war who was held captive in North Vietnam for more than five years.

"The North Vietnamese prime minister had a dinner— I was leaving the next day—and he said if I wanted to take McCain on my flight, it could be arranged," Kissinger told me. At the time, McCain, a naval aviator, had been held prisoner by North Vietnam for five years. He was considered by his captors to be their most cherished prize, because his father, John S. McCain Sr., was the admiral in charge of U.S. operations in the Vietnam theater. Each Christmas during his son's captivity, the senior McCain would travel to the northernmost point of the DMZ to be close to his son. The younger McCain was held in the notorious prison known as the Hanoi Hilton, where he was regularly tortured.

"I told him that I won't take McCain or anyone else on my plane," Kissinger recalled. "The prisoner release would have to happen on a schedule previously agreed. Somehow McCain heard about this and months later, at the White House reception for returned prisoners, he said to me, 'I want to thank you for saving my honor.' What McCain did not tell me at that time was that he had refused to be released two years earlier unless all were released with him. It was better for him to remain in jail in order to preserve his honor and American honor than to come home on my plane."

This behavior was in character for McCain, who, though hot-tempered and imperfect in various ways, was an exemplar of fortitude, courage, and enlightened patriotism across his long career in public service.

I mentioned this story to McCain that same summer, in a hotel suite in Cincinnati. His campaign had already taken on a quixotic feel; McCain's opponent, Barack Obama, was well on the way to his rendezvous with destiny. McCain, for his part, had just chosen Sarah Palin to be his running mate. At the time of this meeting, I had already known McCain for several years; he was the sort of politician who collected reporters, who in turn found him irresistibly interesting and entertaining.

I remember this meeting for two reasons. The first was that it took place on the same day as Senator Obama's speech to 200,000 mesmerized Germans at the Brandenburg

Gate in Berlin, an extraordinary turnout. McCain was flummoxed that an American presidential candidate, so recently unknown, could beguile Europe in this way. McCain had a question for me about Obama: "Did he really appoint a transition team?" I told him he had. McCain shook his head and held his tongue.

The second reason is that McCain was joined in Cincinnati by his Sancho Panza, Senator Lindsey Graham of South Carolina. The two were inseparable. They shared an ideology of free markets, human-rights advocacy, American interventionism, and democracy evangelism. Graham derived meaning from his closeness to McCain— he was, in many ways, Graham's north star—and McCain enjoyed Graham's cleverness and insouciance, as well as his loyalty. The campaign understood Graham to be a kind of flotation device, buoying McCain at a time when not much was going well. And so Graham's role during our conversation was to make jokes and say the things McCain could not, or would not, say. "I guess the community organizer is organizing all of Germany today," Graham said, referring to Obama. "He can give a speech, but what has he accomplished in his life? Zero, nada, nothing." It was Graham's idea, that afternoon, to take McCain to a German restaurant for lunch.

"Lindsey gets upset easily," McCain said, smiling. "Obama could endorse him and give him his winning lottery ticket and Lindsey would find a way to be angry about it." When McCain stepped away for a moment to take a call, I asked Graham what drew him to McCain, other than ideological compatibility. "He's the greatest living American, I swear," Graham said. "He was a POW for five and a half years. They broke half the bones in his body. His bravery, his patriotism—he never broke, not for a second. He's been to hell and back. He paid the price for our freedom." Graham seemed to me bleedingly sincere in his hero worship.

I had not, until then, spent much time talking to McCain about his Vietnam experience. He was never interested in self-analysis. "Stop trying to get me on the couch, you shit," he once snapped at me. But when he came back to the room, I asked him how he understood his Vietnam captivity. How did it shape his views? Did he think about it much when he was younger?

Pay attention to this answer, because it is relevant to our ultimate subject, which is the character of Donald Trump.

McCain said that as a recently released POW, he had been mostly concerned about Vietnam's impact on America's morale. "At that time, I thought about how divided the country was," he said. "You know, that was bothersome to me. The treatment of veterans—the only heroes were the POWs, people who had gotten captured, and in all due respect to us, that's not the object of warfare, to get captured."

I should not have expected anything but self-deprecation. His answer wasn't inaccurate: Vietnam was an unpopular war, and many Americans who could not bring themselves to hold Vietnam-era soldiers in high esteem still felt comfortable respecting, or at least pitying, former POWs. But though he was correct analytically, and though the modesty seemed sincere, it was still a preposterous answer. Prisoners of war in Vietnam—especially those singled out by the North Vietnamese for the harshest possible torture—were men confronting the most acute physical, emotional, and mental challenges. Those who withstood the pressure, who provided comfort to their comrades, who waited their turn for release, and who generally kept their honor were among the most heroic men to ever wear an American uniform.

It would have been very difficult to find someone who disagreed with this notion. Very difficult, that is, until the rise of Donald Trump.

BEFORE THE SUMMER OF 2015, I thought I had a basic understanding of political physics. It was my job to understand how politics works, and how voters think. Before 2015, it was a truism, too obvious to bother stating, that no candidate for public office could ever disparage America's men and women in uniform and survive politically. But on Saturday, July 18, at a forum for Christian conservatives in Iowa, Donald Trump, then one of several candidates for the Republican presidential nomination, overthrew this understanding. It was at this forum that

Trump said of McCain, "He's not a war hero. He is a war hero because he was captured. I like people who weren't captured."

This was a terrible thing to say. John McCain could downplay his heroism; that was his right. But Donald Trump? Donald Trump, whose bone spurs kept him out of the draft? Donald Trump, who said that avoiding STDs in the 1990s was his own personal Vietnam? Donald Trump had no right to criticize John McCain's war record.

I was one of the large number of journalists who hadn't taken Trump's candidacy seriously at first. It was too improbable. He was a racist, a misogynist, a megalomaniac, a *reality-television star*. America wouldn't elect such a man. Trump's odious qualities were even acknowledged in Republican circles, and especially among the field of 2016 Republican contenders. Lindsey Graham was one of those contenders. During the campaign, Graham referred to Trump variously as a "xenophobe" and a "bigot." In this, he was echoing McCain, who understood Trump well and had no patience for him.

I ran into Graham shortly after Trump had disparaged McCain's service. Graham was on fire. "This man"—Trump—"doesn't represent any of the values I hold dear," he said. "He doesn't represent the values of our men and women in uniform, he does not represent the flag, he does not represent the values of patriotic Americans. I wish he would just disappear." In May of 2016, Graham tweeted,

A

"If we nominate Trump, we will get destroyed . . . And we will deserve it."

But Graham, it turned out, misunderstood the Republican electorate. Because what happened after Trump insulted McCain still has the capacity to shock—or shock me, at least—almost a decade later. After Trump made this terrible remark, he didn't slip in the polls. He was not exiled by his party. He actually gained in popularity. I couldn't understand it. I understood how his anti-Mexican racism, and his sexism, might work in his favor, because there existed constituencies within the Republican base for such sentiments. But anti-military sentiment? Anti-POW sentiment? It just didn't track.

Much later on, after I came to understand this new reality (even without being able to explain it), I ran into Graham. By this time, McCain had died, Trump was president, and Graham had a new north star. His conversion to Trumpism was surprising even to those who thought they knew him well.

By late 2018, Graham was a Trump confidant. I didn't see much of him anymore, but when I ran into him that day, I asked him how he could be simultaneously loyal to the memory of John McCain and the reality of Donald Trump. "Look," he said, "I ran for president and lost. He ran for president and won. That's the deal."

But listen to the way he talks about McCain, I said. Look at the things he's done. After McCain died, earlier that summer, Trump had initially refused to lower the flags at the White House in his memory. How could Graham abide that?

"Jeff, if you know about me, you know that I need to be relevant," he said, without defensiveness. "You know who I was just on the phone with?"

Let me guess.

"Donald Trump is the president of the United States," he said. "That's the truth. You think I'm going to go into exile?"

Across Washington, men and women without honor had made this awful compromise. Even after we as a country learned so much more about Donald Trump—about his un-American contempt for the Constitution, about his long history as a sexual miscreant, about his oft-spoken desire to deploy the U.S. military against Americans, and about his unnatural love of dictators from Pyongyang to Moscow—Washington was filled with people who had made their peace with this man, for low, contemptible reasons. John McCain once told me that he liked to think that "in the toughest moments I'd do the right thing, but you never know until you're tested."

Over the past eight years, too many people have failed the test.

THE FIRST ARTICLE IN this collection was published in 2019. It is a profile of James Mattis, the retired Marine

Corps general who became Trump's first secretary of defense. Mattis is the most revered living Marine. I first met him in Iraq, where his men worshipped him. He is a philosopher and a killer. Trump hired him in part because he heard that his nickname was "Mad Dog" (it isn't). What Trump didn't understand about Mattis—what Trump didn't understand about most American flag officers—is that they work for our constitutional ideals and for the American people, not for the president. Mattis eventually fell out with Trump, and this piece represents my arduous attempt to get Mattis to tell me what he really thought of his ex-boss. In extended conversations, on long walks along the Columbia River in Washington State, Mattis gave me broad hints about what he believed, but it wasn't until the summer of 2020, when Trump tried to invoke the Insurrection Act in order to deploy U.S. soldiers against American citizens, that Mattis expressed himself with complete frankness. You'll find what he truly thought of Trump in the second piece in this volume.

The third piece is about John McCain, written shortly after he died. It represents my effort to capture what was so unique about his character. The fourth piece is the most controversial in this collection. The headline we gave the article, when it appeared in September of 2020, was "Trump: Americans Who Died in War Are 'Losers' and 'Suckers.'" In this article, I reported on the many times Trump has disparaged those who serve (including and especially John

McCain). I reported the previously untold story of Trump's visit to Arlington National Cemetery on Memorial Day 2017 with his then–chief of staff, John Kelly, a retired Marine general whose son was killed in Afghanistan. Trump, while standing next to Robert Kelly's grave, turned to his father and said, "I don't get it. What was in it for them?"

The article immediately had an impact. Trump saw it as a challenge to his reelection chances, and he went all-out, condemning me, *The Atlantic*, and anyone who stood by us. He attacked people who he assumed were my sources. He accused me of fabricating the crucial story, in which he referred to American soldiers buried in a cemetery in France as "suckers" and "losers." When a Fox News reporter, Jennifer Griffin, confirmed the story, he called on the network to fire her. Much later, John Kelly confirmed to CNN's Jake Tapper the "suckers and losers" story I'd first reported. Suffice it to say that my sources knew what they were talking about.

The story may or may not have changed voters' minds, but I was glad to have provided this information to our readers. This piece exposed Trump as a coward incapable of understanding selflessness or service.

The fifth piece, "The Patriot," is in some ways the heart of this book. The patriot in question is General Mark Milley, the four-star Army general unlucky enough to have served as chairman of the Joint Chiefs of Staff during the last two years of Trump's presidential term. I was fascinated by Milley because, among other things, he learned the hard way (as you will see) about the nature of Donald Trump's character, but, unlike so many others in Washington, he took his new knowledge to heart. In so doing, he may have saved the republic.

At *The Atlantic*, we've been preoccupied with the subject of political complicity. Anne Applebaum, an *Atlantic* staff writer and a Pulitzer Prize–winning historian, wrote in the summer of 2020 that "we all feel the urge to conform; it is the most normal of human desires." It was her insight that acquiescence and collaboration, not principled dissent, is the default and very human posture of most people, including most politicians. When Trump started winning, it was so much easier, and so much more lucrative, for Republican politicians to fall in line, rather than argue against their party's clear authoritarian turn.

There have been a few noteworthy dissenters in the Trump-era Republican Party. One of those is Mitt Romney, the Utah senator, who has been so ably profiled by my colleague McKay Coppins. Another dissenter, one I've written about over the past few years, is the now-former Republican congressman Adam Kinzinger, who gave up his seat in the House rather than compromise his values. Our conversations have given me some understanding of what it takes to go against the crowd.

Kinzinger, like Lindsey Graham, was a protégé of John McCain's. Unlike Graham, Kinzinger, a former U.S. Air

Force pilot, stayed true to his mentor. I first met him in 2014, when we were both part of a delegation McCain brought to the Munich Security Conference, which is something like the Burning Man of defense conclaves. McCain was in many ways the mayor of this conference. Everyone sought him out for advice, favors, blessings, and photos. He enjoyed himself very much, often at the expense of his delegation. During one roundtable discussion with the national security adviser of India, McCain introduced Kinzinger by saying, "This is Adam Kinzinger. He's Henry Kissinger's bastard son." The Indian national security adviser appeared to believe him.

Later that night, a small group of us visited a Munich beer hall. Memory is a bit hazy here, but I do remember a large, drunk German falling on Lindsey Graham. Also with us was Mike Pompeo, who was then a congressman from Kansas, and who would later go on to become a more or less loyal follower of Trump as well. But back then, Kinzinger was in complete alignment with Graham and Pompeo. "I just assumed that we would be the core of people holding the torch for American leadership" in the world, he said.

Kinzinger would eventually become an apostate, breaking with Graham and Pompeo, and joining the committee investigating the January 6 insurrection. Liz Cheney was the only other Republican on the committee. Neither is in Congress any longer. I asked Kinzinger recently if

A

he thought he had been naive about the people who now lead the party. "You know, you always think that everyone has a red line," he said. "No matter how much politics a person can play, there's a red line that people can't cross." Kinzinger talked about his shock at Trump's disregard for the Constitution, and in particular his disregard for the military. He never thought Republicans would elect a person who expressed disrespect for national service. "I was naive. There are some people who only care about access to power. I'm still coming to terms with this." He went on to say, "I don't have a tribe. The good thing is, I don't really care."

I sensed that there was a bit of bravado in his answer. It is not easy to go against your group, your party, your tribe. Which is why most people don't. In recent years, too many people in Washington have failed the test of character and leadership. In the following chapters, you'll meet a handful who did not.

Jeffrey Goldberg
April 2024

A

# THE MAN WHO COULDN'T
# TAKE IT ANYMORE

*October 2019*

ON DECEMBER 19 OF LAST year, Admiral Michael Mullen, the former chairman of the Joint Chiefs of Staff, met James Mattis for lunch at the Pentagon. Mattis was a day away from resigning as Donald Trump's secretary of defense, but he tends to keep his own counsel, and he did not suggest to Mullen, his friend and former commander, that he was thinking of leaving.

But Mullen did think Mattis appeared unusually afflicted that day. Mattis often seemed burdened in his role. His aides and friends say he found the president to be of limited cognitive ability, and of generally dubious character. Now Mattis was becoming more and more isolated in the administration, especially since the defenestration of his closest Cabinet ally, the former secretary of state Rex Tillerson, several months earlier. Mattis and Tillerson had together smothered some of Trump's more extreme and imprudent ideas. But now Mattis was operating without cover. Trump was turning on him publicly; two months earlier, he had speculated that Mattis might be a Democrat and said, in reference to NATO, "I think

I know more about it than he does." (Mattis, as a Marine general, once served as the supreme allied commander in charge of NATO transformation.)

Mullen told me recently that service in this administration comes with a unique set of hazards, and that Mattis was not unaware of these hazards. "I think back to his 'Hold the line' talk, the one that was captured on video," Mullen said, referring to an impromptu 2017 encounter between Mattis and U.S. troops stationed in Jordan that became a YouTube sensation. In the video, Mattis tells the soldiers, "Our country right now, it's got problems we don't have in the military. You just hold the line until our country gets back to understanding and respecting each other and showing it." Mullen said: "He obviously found himself in a challenging environment."

Mullen's concern for Mattis was shared by many other generals and admirals, active duty and retired, who worried that sustained exposure to Trump would destroy their friend, who is perhaps the most revered living marine. Mattis had maintained his dignity in perilous moments, even as his fellow Cabinet officials were relinquishing theirs. At a ritualized praise session at the White House in June 2017, as the vice president and other Cabinet members abased themselves before the president, Mattis would offer only this generic—but, given the circumstances, dissident—thought: "It's an honor to represent the men and women of the Department of Defense.

A

We are grateful for the sacrifices our people are making in order to strengthen our military, so our diplomats always negotiate from a position of strength."

To some of his friends, though, Mattis was beginning to place his reputation at risk. He had, in the fall of 2018, acquiesced to Trump's deployment of troops to the U.S.-Mexico border, and he was becoming contemptuous of a Pentagon press corps that was trying to perform its duty in difficult circumstances.

By last December, Mattis was facing the most urgent crisis of his nearly two years in the Cabinet. Trump had just announced, contrary to his administration's stated policy, that he would withdraw all American troops from Syria, where they were fighting the Islamic State. This sudden (and ultimately reversed) policy shift posed a dire challenge to Mattis's beliefs. He had spent much of his career as a fighter in the Middle East. He had battled Islamist extremists and understood the danger they represented. He believed that a retreat from Syria would threaten the security of American troops elsewhere in the region, and would especially threaten America's allies in the anti-ISIS coalition. These allies would, in Mattis's view, feel justifiably betrayed by Trump's decision.

"I had no idea that he was on the precipice of resigning," Mullen told me. "But I know how strongly he believes in alliances. The practical reasons become moral reasons. Most of us believe that we've moved on as a country from being able to do it alone. We may have had dreams about this in 1992 or 1993, but we've moved on. We have to have friends and supporters. And we're talking about Jim Mattis. He's not going to change his view on this. He's not going to leave friends and allies on the battlefield."

That afternoon, Mattis called John Kelly, the former Marine general who was then nearing the end of his calamitous run as Trump's chief of staff. "I need an hour with the boss," Mattis said.

The next day, he met Trump in the Oval Office. Mattis made his case for keeping troops in Syria. Trump rejected his arguments. Thirty minutes into the conversation, Mattis told the president, "You're going to have to get the next secretary of defense to lose to ISIS. I'm not going to do it." He handed Trump his resignation letter, a letter that would soon become one of the most famous documents of the Trump presidency thus far.

Here is where I am compelled to note that I did not learn any of these details from Mattis himself. Nor did I learn them from his new book, *Call Sign Chaos: Learning to Lead*, which he wrote with the former Marine officer Bing West. The book is an instructive and entertaining leadership manual for executives, managers, and military officers. Mattis is a gifted storyteller, and his advice will be useful to anyone who runs anything. The book is not, however, an account of his time in service to the 45th president.

A

I've known Mattis for many years, and we spent several hours in conversation this summer, at his home in Richland, Washington, and at the Hoover Institution, on the campus of Stanford University. In these conversations, we discussed the qualities of effective leadership, the workings of command-and-feedback loops, the fragility of what he calls the American experiment, fishing the Columbia River, the *Meditations* of Marcus Aurelius, and many other topics. But about Trump he was mainly silent. I caught glimpses of anger and incredulity, to be sure. But Mattis is a disciplined man. While discipline is an admirable quality, in my conversations with Mattis I found it exasperating, because I believe that the American people should hear his answer to this question: Is Donald Trump fit for command?

He should answer the question well before November 3, 2020. Mattis is in an unparalleled position to provide a definitive answer. During moments of high tension with North Korea, he had worried that being out of reach of the president for more than a few seconds constituted a great risk. No one, with the possible exception of John Kelly, has a better understanding of Donald Trump's capacities and inclinations, particularly in the realm of national security, than James Mattis.

I made this argument to him during an interview at his home, a modest townhouse in a modest development in a modest town. Mattis, who is 69, is single, and has always been so. His house serves mainly as a library of the literature of war and diplomacy, and as a museum of ceremonial daggers, the residue of a lifetime of official visits to army headquarters across the Middle East. The decor reminded me of one of his sayings: "Be polite, be professional, but have a plan to kill everybody you meet."

I knew that this would be a Gallipoli of an interview, and that Mattis would be playing the role of the Ottoman gunners. But I had to try.

"When you go out on book tour," I said, "people are going to want you to say things you don't want to say." I mentioned a scene from the book, one that concerned an ultimately successful effort to untangle a traffic jam of armored vehicles in Iraq. I noted that while this story is an edifying case study in effective leadership, it is not necessarily the sort of story that people want from him right now.

"Yeah," he said.

"You're prepared for that? For people wanting you to talk about Trump?"

He paused.

"Do you know the French concept of *devoir de réserve*?" he asked.

I did not, I said.

"The duty of silence. If you leave an administration, you owe some silence. When you leave an administration over clear policy differences, you need to give the people who are still there as much opportunity as possible to

A

defend the country. They still have the responsibility of protecting this great big experiment of ours. I know the malevolence some people feel for this country, and we have to give the people who are protecting us some time to carry out their duties without me adding my criticism to the cacophony that is right now so poisonous."

"But duty manifests in other ways," I argued. "You have a First Amendment guarantee to speak your mind—"

"Absolutely."

"And don't you have a duty to warn the country if it is endangered by its leader?"

"I didn't cook up a convenient tradition here," he said. "You don't endanger the country by attacking the elected commander in chief. I may not like a commander in chief one fricking bit, but our system puts the commander in chief there, and to further weaken him when we're up against real threats—I mean, we could be at war on the Korean peninsula, every time they start launching something."

The subject of North Korea represented my best chance to wrench a direct answer from Mattis. I had collected some of Trump's more repellent tweets, and read aloud the one that I thought might overwhelm his defenses. It is a tweet almost without peer in the canon:

North Korea fired off some small weapons, which disturbed some of my people, and others, but not me. I have confidence that Chairman Kim will keep his promise to me, & also smiled when he called Swampman Joe Biden a low IQ individual, & worse. Perhaps that's sending me a signal?

Mattis looked at his hands. Finally he said, "Any Marine general or any other senior servant of the people of the United States would find that, to use a mild euphemism, counterproductive and beneath the dignity of the presidency."

He went on, "Let me put it this way. I've written an entire book built on the principles of respecting your troops, respecting each other, respecting your allies. Isn't it pretty obvious how I would feel about something like that?"

It is. When *Call Sign Chaos* is refracted through the prism of our hallucinatory political moment, it becomes something more than a primer for middle managers. The book is many things, apart from a meditation on leadership. It is the autobiography of a war fighter, and also an extended argument for a forceful, confident, alliance-centered U.S. foreign policy. Read another way, though, it is mainly a 100,000-word subtweet.

When I mentioned this notion to Mattis, he looked at me curiously. He is not closely acquainted with the language of social media. When I explained what a subtweet is, he said, "Well, you saw that my resignation letter is in the book."

It comes near the end. Each chapter contains a lesson about personal leadership, or American leadership, or some

A

combination of the two: "Coach and encourage, don't berate, least of all in public." "Public humiliation does not change our friends' behavior or attitudes in a positive way." "Operations occur at the speed of trust." "Nations with allies thrive, and those without wither." And then comes the resignation letter, a repudiation of a man who models none of Mattis's principles:

> While the US remains the indispensable nation in the free world, we cannot protect our interests or serve that role effectively without maintaining strong alliances and showing respect to those allies . . .

> My views on treating allies with respect and also being clear-eyed about both malign actors and strategic competitors are strongly held and informed by over four decades of immersion in these issues. We must do everything possible to advance an international order that is most conducive to our security, prosperity and values, and we are strengthened in this effort by the solidarity of our alliances.

> Because you have the right to have a Secretary of Defense whose views are better aligned with yours on these and other subjects, I believe it is right for me to step down from my position.

"I had no choice but to leave," he told me. "That's why the letter is in the book. I want people to understand why I couldn't stay. I've been informed by four decades of experience, and I just couldn't connect the dots anymore."

Later, during a long walk along the Columbia River, I gave it another go, asking him to describe in broad terms the nature of Trump's leadership abilities. "I'm happy to talk about leadership," he said. "My model—one of my models—is George Washington. Washington's idea of leadership was that first you listen, then you learn, then you help, and only then do you lead. It is a somewhat boring progression, but it's useful. What you try to do in that learning phase is find common ground."

"So on one end of the spectrum is George Washington, and at the other end is Donald Trump?"

Mattis smiled. "It's a beautiful river, isn't it?" he said. "I used to swim it all the time when I was a kid. Strong current."

In mid-August I checked in with Mattis, to see whether events over the summer—Trump's attack on four congresswomen of color; his attack on Representative Elijah Cummings; his attacks on other minorities; his endorsement-by-tweet of the North Korean dictator's "great and beautiful vision" for his country; the El Paso massacre, conducted by a white supremacist whose words echoed those often used by Trump and his supporters when discussing immigration—might have led him to

A

reconsider his decorous approach to public criticism of the president.

About El Paso he said: "You know, on that day we were all Hispanics. That's the way we have to think about this. If it happens to any one of us, it happens to all of us."

But about this treacherous political moment?

"You've got to avoid looking at what's happening in isolation from everything else," he said. "We can't hold what Trump is doing in isolation. We've got to address the things that put him there in the first place." Mattis speaks often about affection: the affection that commanders feel for their soldiers, and that soldiers ought to feel for one another—and the affection that Americans should feel for one another and for their country but often, these days, don't. "'With malice toward none, with charity for all,'" he said. "Lincoln said that in the middle of a war. In the middle of a war! He could see beyond the hatred of the moment."

I thought back to what he'd told me earlier in the summer, when I had asked him to describe something Trump could say or do that would trigger him to launch a frontal attack on the president. He'd demurred, as I had expected. But then he'd issued a caveat: "There is a period in which I owe my silence. It's not eternal. It's not going to be forever."

# A THREAT TO THE
# CONSTITUTION

*June 2020*

JAMES MATTIS, THE ESTEEMED MARINE general who resigned as secretary of defense in December 2018 to protest Donald Trump's Syria policy, has, ever since, kept studiously silent about Trump's performance as president. But he has now broken his silence, writing an extraordinary broadside in which he denounces the president for dividing the nation, and accuses him of ordering the U.S. military to violate the constitutional rights of American citizens.

"I have watched this week's unfolding events, angry and appalled," Mattis writes. "The words 'Equal Justice Under Law' are carved in the pediment of the United States Supreme Court. This is precisely what protesters are rightly demanding. It is a wholesome and unifying demand—one that all of us should be able to get behind. We must not be distracted by a small number of lawbreakers. The protests are defined by tens of thousands of people of conscience who are insisting that we live up to our values—our values as people and our values as a nation." He goes on, "We must reject and hold accountable those in office who would make a mockery of our Constitution."

In his j'accuse, Mattis excoriates the president for setting Americans against one another.

"Donald Trump is the first president in my lifetime who does not try to unite the American people—does not even pretend to try. Instead, he tries to divide us," Mattis writes. "We are witnessing the consequences of three years of this deliberate effort. We are witnessing the consequences of three years without mature leadership. We can unite without him, drawing on the strengths inherent in our civil society. This will not be easy, as the past few days have shown, but we owe it to our fellow citizens; to past generations that bled to defend our promise; and to our children."

He goes on to contrast the American ethos of unity with Nazi ideology. "Instructions given by the military departments to our troops before the Normandy invasion reminded soldiers that 'The Nazi slogan for destroying us . . . was "Divide and Conquer." Our American answer is "In Union there is Strength."' We must summon that unity to surmount this crisis—confident that we are better than our politics."

Mattis's dissatisfaction with Trump was no secret inside the Pentagon. But after his resignation, he argued publicly—and to great criticism—that it would be inappropriate and counterproductive for a former general, and a former Cabinet official, to criticize a sitting president. Doing so, he said, would threaten the apolitical nature of the military. When I interviewed him last year on this subject, he said, "When you leave an administration over clear policy differences, you need to give the people who are still there as much opportunity as possible to defend the country. They still have the responsibility of protecting this great big experiment of ours." He did add, however: "There is a period in which I owe my silence. It's not eternal. It's not going to be forever."

That period is now definitively over. Mattis reached the conclusion this past weekend that the American experiment is directly threatened by the actions of the president he once served. In his statement, Mattis makes it clear that the president's response to the police killing of George Floyd, and the ensuing protests, triggered this public condemnation.

"When I joined the military, some 50 years ago," he writes, "I swore an oath to support and defend the Constitution. Never did I dream that troops taking that same oath would be ordered under any circumstance to violate the Constitutional rights of their fellow citizens—much less to provide a bizarre photo op for the elected commander-in-chief, with military leadership standing alongside."

He goes on to implicitly criticize the current secretary of defense, Mark Esper, and other senior officials as well. "We must reject any thinking of our cities as a 'battlespace' that our uniformed military is called upon to 'dominate.' At home, we should use our military only when requested to do so, on very rare occasions, by state governors. Militarizing our response, as we witnessed in Washington, D.C., sets up a conflict—a false conflict—between the military and civilian society. It erodes the moral ground that ensures a trusted bond between men and women in uniform and the society they are sworn to protect, and of which they themselves are a part. Keeping public order rests with civilian state and local leaders who best understand their communities and are answerable to them."

Here is the text of the complete statement.

*In Union There Is Strength*

I have watched this week's unfolding events, angry and appalled. The words "Equal Justice Under Law" are carved in the pediment of the United States Supreme Court. This is precisely what protesters are rightly demanding. It is a wholesome and unifying demand—one that all of us should be able to get behind. We must not be distracted by a small number of lawbreakers. The protests are defined by tens of thousands of people of conscience who are insisting that we live up to our values—our values as people and our values as a nation.

When I joined the military, some 50 years ago, I swore an oath to support and defend the Constitution. Never did I dream that troops taking that same oath would be ordered under any circumstance to violate the Constitutional rights of their fellow citizens—much less to provide a bizarre photo op for the elected commander-in-chief, with military leadership standing alongside.

We must reject any thinking of our cities as a "battlespace" that our uniformed military is called upon to "dominate." At home, we should use our military only when requested to do so, on very rare occasions, by state governors. Militarizing our response, as we witnessed in Washington, D.C., sets up a conflict—a false conflict—between the military and civilian society. It erodes the moral ground that ensures a trusted bond between men and women in uniform and the society they are sworn to protect, and of which they themselves are a part. Keeping public order rests with civilian state and local leaders who best understand their communities and are answerable to them.

James Madison wrote in Federalist 41 that "America united with a handful of troops, or without a single soldier, exhibits a more forbidding posture to foreign ambition than America disunited, with a hundred thousand veterans ready for combat." We do not need to militarize our response to protests. We need to unite around a common purpose. And it starts by guaranteeing that all of us are equal before the law.

A

Instructions given by the military departments to our troops before the Normandy invasion reminded soldiers that "The Nazi slogan for destroying us . . . was 'Divide and Conquer.' Our American answer is 'In Union there is Strength.'" We must summon that unity to surmount this crisis—confident that we are better than our politics.

Donald Trump is the first president in my lifetime who does not try to unite the American people—does not even pretend to try. Instead he tries to divide us. We are witnessing the consequences of three years of this deliberate effort. We are witnessing the consequences of three years without mature leadership. We can unite without him, drawing on the strengths inherent in our civil society. This will not be easy, as the past few days have shown, but we owe it to our fellow citizens; to past generations that bled to defend our promise; and to our children.

We can come through this trying time stronger, and with a renewed sense of purpose and respect for one another. The pandemic has shown us that it is not only our troops who are willing to offer the ultimate sacrifice for the safety of the community. Americans in hospitals, grocery stores, post offices, and elsewhere have put their lives on the line in order to serve their fellow citizens and their country. We know that we are better than the abuse of executive authority that we witnessed in Lafayette Square. We must reject and hold accountable those in office who would make a mockery of our Constitution. At the same time, we must remember Lincoln's "better angels," and listen to them, as we work to unite.

Only by adopting a new path—which means, in truth, returning to the original path of our founding ideals—will we again be a country admired and respected at home and abroad.

A

# THE ANNE FRANK TEST

*August 2018*

A DECADE AGO, ON ONE of his seemingly countless visits to Iraq, John McCain, who was generally immune to the charms of introspection—"Stop trying to get me on the couch, you shit," he once said, smiling, when I tried to encourage him toward self-analysis—talked about the dominion of human cowardice, and the story of Anne Frank, in a way that I found startling.

We had been discussing the American war in Iraq, which he supported steadfastly, even after everything went sideways. The cause, he said, was just. The execution, at least until the troop surge of 2007, was a disgrace, but this didn't move him off his principles. "I hated Saddam," he said. "He ruled through murder. Didn't we learn from Hitler that we can't let that happen?" His hatred of Saddam Hussein, like his hatred for all dictators, burned hot; his contempt for Donald Rumsfeld, George W. Bush's first defense secretary, was ice-cold. It was Rumsfeld's arrogance and incompetence, McCain believed, that helped discredit the American invasion. "He was the worst," McCain said.

I offered a qualified dissent in response. I supported the invasion for more or less the same reason McCain did—I wanted to see the Kurdish people, the preeminent victims of Saddam's genocidal fury, suffer no more. But unlike McCain, I had come to believe that the theory of the American case was no match for heartbreaking Middle East reality. I wasn't sure that even the most perspicacious secretary of defense could successfully lead an effort to renovate a despotic Middle Eastern country. I suggested to McCain that this sort of grandiose undertaking was not necessarily a core competency of the United States. "But genocide!" he said. "Genocide!" His argument was not only concise, but morally superior. Not analytically superior, but morally, no doubt.

We spoke every so often about the Holocaust, and its supposed lessons (one lesson, he told me once, in a mainly, though not entirely, devilish way, was that Jews should be well armed). He said that, in the post-Holocaust world, all civilized people, and the governments of all civilized nations, should be intolerant of leaders who commit verified acts of genocide. That, he suggested, is the most salient lesson of all.

I told him then that he would most definitely pass the Anne Frank test. He was unfamiliar with the concept (mildly surprising, given that his best friend was Joe Lieberman). The Anne Frank test, something I learned from a Holocaust survivor almost 40 years ago, is actually a single question: Which non-Jewish friends would risk their lives to hide us should the Nazis ever return?

McCain laughed at the compliment. Then he became serious. "I like to think that in the toughest moments I'd do the right thing, but you never know until you're tested." I found this to be an absurd thing for him to say. Few men had been tested like John McCain; few men have passed these tests in the manner of John McCain. Of all the many stories of McCain's heroism in Vietnamese captivity, the one I've always found most affecting is this one: When presented with the opportunity to be freed—he was the son of an important admiral, and his release would constitute a propaganda victory for the North Vietnamese—McCain demurred; it was not his turn (prisoners were generally released based on their time in captivity), and he would not skip to the head of the line. When he rejected the Vietnamese offer, he knew that intense torture would be his reward. And he did it anyway. His sense of honor would allow him to do nothing else.

I pressed him on this point. "I've failed enough in my life to know that it's always an option," he said. "I like to think I would do what it takes, but fear will make you do terrible things."

I couldn't stand it anymore. "I'm pretty sure you'd kill Nazis to defend Anne Frank," I said.

He smiled. "It would be an honor and a privilege."

John McCain possessed many sterling qualities; two of the most admirable were on display in this conversation. The first was his visceral antipathy for powerful men who abuse powerless people. A few years ago, I asked him about a fight he was then having with President Barack Obama. McCain wanted Obama to supply Ukraine with weapons it could deploy against Russian invaders. Obama, quite logically, believed that these weapons would be ineffective against the Russian juggernaut, and might actually provoke Vladimir Putin into even more aggressive action. McCain understood the possible ramifications of a decision to arm the Ukrainians. But his sense of honor—and his Hemingway-influenced romantic fatalism—led him to a different conclusion.

"When people want to fight for their freedom, we have to be there with them." As one of his aides later explained, "He believes it's better to die fighting than just die."

I asked McCain, *Is this the American way?* "It should be," he said. "It always should be." (McCain's amanuensis, his former chief of staff Mark Salter, told me recently, when I asked him if McCain is more frustrated by Putin's existence or by the fact that some Americans—I had in mind one American in particular—don't seem to understand Putin's nature, "There's always a Putin somewhere in the world, and you're meant to oppose them with all the skills God gave you.")

The second quality on display in our conversation was self-doubt—or, at the very least, self-knowledge. It is almost impossible, in our era, for politicians to keep from becoming hollowed out (assuming they weren't hollow to begin with). There is no reward in American politics for public displays of

A

self-awareness or self-criticism. And yet, John McCain understood human nature, and his own nature, enough to state the plausible: that in moments of great testing, it is possible for any human, including the bravest human, to fail.

McCain, of course, failed in various ways, large and small. I think that many of his failures will be forgotten by history, except for the fact that he tended to catalog them himself, and then recite them publicly.

Once, on a lightning-fast trip to Hungary (all of his trips seemed lightning-fast; as *The Washington Post*'s Josh Rogin recalls, McCain's aides would refer to his overseas adventures as Bataan Death Marches), I raised the subject of imperfection—not his, but America's. McCain was visiting Budapest to buttress the democratic opposition there, and to fire a warning shot at the country's autocratically minded president. I asked him if it ever felt hypocritical to argue for a set of values that we live in America only aspirationally. "We get things wrong all the time," he said. "It's true. But the ideals are great, they're perfect. They're something to aim for."

John McCain was far from perfect. But as his former campaign adviser Steve Schmidt said Saturday night, shortly after McCain died, "He perfectly loved this country."

A man apparently devoid of any redeeming qualities currently occupies the Oval Office. It is important to remember that America is also capable of producing leaders like John McCain.

# LOSERS AND SUCKERS

*September 2020*

WHEN PRESIDENT DONALD TRUMP CANCELED a visit to the Aisne-Marne American Cemetery, near Paris in 2018, he blamed rain for the last-minute decision, saying that "the helicopter couldn't fly" and that the Secret Service wouldn't drive him there. Neither claim was true.

Trump rejected the idea of the visit because he feared his hair would become disheveled in the rain, and because he did not believe it important to honor American war dead, according to four people with firsthand knowledge of the discussion that day. In a conversation with senior staff members on the morning of the scheduled visit, Trump said, "Why should I go to that cemetery? It's filled with losers." In a separate conversation on the same trip, Trump referred to the more than 1,800 Marines who lost their lives at Belleau Wood as "suckers" for getting killed.

Belleau Wood is a consequential battle in American history, and the ground on which it was fought is venerated by the Marine Corps. America and its allies stopped the German advance toward Paris there in the spring of 1918. But Trump, on that same trip, asked aides, "Who were the good guys in this war?" He also said that he didn't understand why the United States would intervene on the side of the Allies.

Trump's understanding of concepts such as patriotism, service, and sacrifice has interested me since he expressed contempt for the war record of the late senator John McCain, who spent more than five years as a prisoner of the North Vietnamese. "He's not a war hero," Trump said in 2015 while running for the Republican nomination for president. "I like people who weren't captured."

There was no precedent in American politics for the expression of this sort of contempt, but the performatively patriotic Trump did no damage to his candidacy by attacking McCain in this manner. Nor did he set his campaign back by attacking the parents of Humayun Khan, an Army captain who was killed in Iraq in 2004.

Trump remained fixated on McCain, one of the few prominent Republicans to continue criticizing him after he won the nomination. When McCain died, in August 2018, Trump told his senior staff, according to three sources with direct knowledge of this event, "We're not going to support that loser's funeral," and he became furious, according to witnesses, when he saw flags lowered to half-staff. "What the fuck are we doing that for? Guy was a fucking loser," the president told aides. Trump was not invited to McCain's funeral. (These sources, and others quoted in this article, spoke on condition of anonymity. The White House did not return earlier calls for comment, but Alyssa Farah, a White House spokesperson, emailed me this statement shortly after this story was posted: "This report is false. President Trump holds the military in the highest regard. He's demonstrated his commitment to them at every turn: delivering on his promise to give our troops a much needed pay raise, increasing military spending, signing critical veterans reforms, and supporting military spouses. This has no basis in fact.")

Trump's understanding of heroism has not evolved since he became president. According to sources with knowledge of the president's views, he seems to genuinely not understand why Americans treat former prisoners of war with respect. Nor does he understand why pilots who are shot down in combat are honored by the military. On at least two occasions since becoming president, according to three sources with direct knowledge of his views, Trump referred to former president George H. W. Bush as a "loser" for being shot down by the Japanese as a Navy pilot in World War II. (Bush escaped capture, but eight other men shot down during the same mission were caught, tortured, and executed by Japanese soldiers.)

When lashing out at critics, Trump often reaches for illogical and corrosive insults, and members of the Bush family have publicly opposed him. But his cynicism about service and heroism extends even to the World War I dead buried outside Paris—people who were killed more than a quarter century before he was born. Trump finds the notion of military service difficult to understand, and the idea of volunteering to serve especially incomprehensible. (The president did not serve in the military; he received a medical deferment from the draft during the Vietnam War because of the alleged presence of bone spurs in his feet. In the 1990s, Trump said his efforts to avoid contracting sexually transmitted diseases constituted his "personal Vietnam.")

On Memorial Day 2017, Trump visited Arlington National Cemetery, a short drive from the White House. He was accompanied on this visit by John Kelly, who was then the secretary of homeland security, and who would, a short time later, be named the White House chief of staff. The two men were set to visit Section 60, the 14-acre area of the cemetery that is the burial ground for those killed in America's most recent wars. Kelly's son Robert is buried in Section 60. A first lieutenant in the Marine Corps, Robert Kelly was killed in 2010 in Afghanistan. He was 29. Trump was meant, on this visit, to join John Kelly in paying respects at his son's grave, and to comfort the families of other fallen service members. But according to sources with knowledge of this visit, Trump, while standing by Robert Kelly's grave, turned directly to his father and said, "I don't get it. What was in it for them?" Kelly (who declined to comment for this story) initially believed, people close to him said, that Trump was making a ham-handed reference to the selflessness of America's all-volunteer force. But later he came to realize that Trump simply does not understand non-transactional life choices.

"He can't fathom the idea of doing something for someone other than himself," one of Kelly's friends, a retired four-star general, told me. "He just thinks that anyone who does anything when there's no direct personal gain to be had is a sucker. There's no money in serving the nation." Kelly's friend went on to say, "Trump can't imagine anyone else's pain. That's why he would say this to the father of a fallen Marine on Memorial Day in the cemetery where he's buried."

I've asked numerous general officers over the past year for their analysis of Trump's seeming contempt for military service. They offer a number of explanations. Some of his cynicism is rooted in frustration, they say. Trump, unlike previous presidents, tends to believe that the military, like other departments of the federal government, is beholden only to him, and not the Constitution. Many senior officers have expressed worry about Trump's understanding of the rules governing the use of the armed forces. This issue came to a head in early June, during demonstrations in Washington, D.C., in response to police killings of Black people. James Mattis, the retired Marine general and former secretary of defense, lambasted Trump at the time for ordering law-enforcement officers to forcibly clear protesters from Lafayette Square, and for using soldiers as props: "When I joined the military, some

50 years ago, I swore an oath to support and defend the Constitution," Mattis wrote. "Never did I dream that troops taking that same oath would be ordered under any circumstance to violate the Constitutional rights of their fellow citizens—much less to provide a bizarre photo op for the elected commander-in-chief, with military leadership standing alongside."

Another explanation is more quotidian, and aligns with a broader understanding of Trump's material-focused worldview. The president believes that nothing is worth doing without the promise of monetary payback, and that talented people who don't pursue riches are "losers." (According to eyewitnesses, after a White House briefing given by the then-chairman of the Joint Chiefs of Staff, General Joe Dunford, Trump turned to aides and said, "That guy is smart. Why did he join the military?")

Yet another, related, explanation concerns what appears to be Trump's pathological fear of appearing to look like a "sucker" himself. His capacious definition of *sucker* includes those who lose their lives in service to their country, as well as those who are taken prisoner, or are wounded in battle. "He has a lot of fear," one officer with firsthand knowledge of Trump's views said. "He doesn't see the heroism in fighting." Several observers told me that Trump is deeply anxious about dying or being disfigured, and this worry manifests itself as disgust for those who have suffered. Trump recently claimed that he has received the bodies of slain service members "many, many" times, but in fact he has traveled to Dover Air Force Base, the transfer point for the remains of fallen service members, only four times since becoming president. In another incident, Trump falsely claimed that he had called "virtually all" of the families of service members who had died during his term, then began rush-shipping condolence letters when families said the president was not telling the truth.

Trump has been, for the duration of his presidency, fixated on staging military parades, but only of a certain sort. In a 2018 White House planning meeting for such an event, Trump asked his staff not to include wounded veterans, on grounds that spectators would feel uncomfortable in the presence of amputees. "Nobody wants to see that," he said.

# THE PATRIOT

*September 2023*

THE MISSILES THAT COMPRISE THE land component of America's nuclear triad are scattered across thousands of square miles of prairie and farmland, mainly in North Dakota, Montana, and Wyoming. About 150 of the roughly 400 Minuteman III intercontinental ballistic missiles currently on alert are dispersed in a wide circle around Minot Air Force Base, in the upper reaches of North Dakota. From Minot, it would take an ICBM about 25 minutes to reach Moscow.

These nuclear weapons are under the control of the 91st Missile Wing of the Air Force Global Strike Command, and it was to the 91st—the "Rough Riders"—that General Mark Milley, the chairman of the Joint Chiefs of Staff, paid a visit in March 2021. I accompanied him on the trip. A little more than two months had passed since the January 6 attack on the Capitol, and America's nuclear arsenal was on Milley's mind.

In normal times, the chairman of the Joint Chiefs, the principal military adviser to the president, is supposed to focus his attention on America's national-security challenges, and on the readiness and lethality of its armed forces. But the first 16 months of Milley's term, a period that ended when Joe Biden succeeded Donald Trump as president, were not normal, because Trump was exceptionally unfit to serve. "For more than 200 years, the assumption in this country was that we would have a stable person as president," one of Milley's mentors, the retired three-star general James Dubik, told me. That this assumption did not hold true during the Trump administration presented a "unique challenge" for Milley, Dubik said.

Milley was careful to refrain from commenting publicly on Trump's cognitive unfitness and moral derangement. In interviews, he would say that it is not the place of the nation's flag officers to discuss the performance of the nation's civilian leaders.

But his views emerged in a number of books published after Trump left office, written by authors who had spoken with Milley, and many other civilian and military officials, on background. In *The Divider*, Peter Baker and Susan Glasser write that Milley believed that Trump was "shameful," and "complicit" in the January 6 attack. They also reported that Milley feared that Trump's "'Hitler-like' embrace of the big lie about the election would prompt the president to seek out a 'Reichstag moment.'"

These views of Trump align with those of many officials who served in his administration. Trump's first secretary of state, Rex Tillerson, considered Trump to be a "fucking moron." John Kelly, the retired Marine general

A

who served as Trump's chief of staff in 2017 and 2018, has said that Trump is the "most flawed person" he's ever met. James Mattis, who is also a retired Marine general and served as Trump's first secretary of defense, has told friends and colleagues that the 45th president was "more dangerous than anyone could ever imagine." It is widely known that Trump's second secretary of defense, Mark Esper, believed that the president didn't understand his own duties, much less the oath that officers swear to the Constitution, or military ethics, or the history of America.

Twenty men have served as the chairman of the Joint Chiefs since the position was created after World War II. Until Milley, none had been forced to confront the possibility that a president would try to foment or provoke a coup in order to illegally remain in office. A plain reading of the record shows that in the chaotic period before and after the 2020 election, Milley did as much as, or more than, any other American to defend the constitutional order, to prevent the military from being deployed against the American people, and to forestall the eruption of wars with America's nuclear-armed adversaries. Along the way, Milley deflected Trump's exhortations to have the U.S. military ignore, and even on occasion commit, war crimes. Milley and other military officers deserve praise for protecting democracy, but their actions should also cause deep unease. In the American system, it is the voters, the courts, and Congress that are meant to serve as checks on a president's behavior, not the generals. Civilians provide direction, funding, and oversight; the military then follows lawful orders.

The difficulty of the task before Milley was captured most succinctly by Lieutenant General H. R. McMaster, the second of Trump's four national security advisers. "As chairman, you swear to support and defend the Constitution of the United States, but what if the commander in chief is undermining the Constitution?" McMaster said to me.

For the actions he took in the last months of the Trump presidency, Milley, whose four-year term as chairman, and 43-year career as an Army officer, will conclude at the end of September, has been condemned by elements of the far right. Kash Patel, whom Trump installed in a senior Pentagon role in the final days of his administration, refers to Milley as "the Kraken of the swamp." Trump himself has accused Milley of treason. Sebastian Gorka, a former Trump White House official, has said that Milley deserves to be placed in "shackles and leg irons." If a second Trump administration were to attempt this, however, the Trumpist faction would be opposed by the large group of ex-Trump-administration officials who believe that the former president continues to pose a unique threat to American democracy, and who believe that Milley is a hero for what he did to protect the country and the Constitution.

"Mark Milley had to contain the impulses of people who wanted to use the United States military in very dangerous ways," Kelly told me. "Mark had a very, very difficult reality to deal with in his first two years as chairman, and he served honorably and well. The president couldn't fathom people who served their nation honorably." Kelly, along with other former administration officials, has argued that Trump has a contemptuous view of the military, and that this contempt made it extraordinarily difficult to explain to Trump such concepts as honor, sacrifice, and duty.

Robert Gates, who served as secretary of defense under Presidents George W. Bush and Barack Obama, told me that no Joint Chiefs chairman has ever been tested in the manner Milley was. "General Milley has done an extraordinary job under the most extraordinary of circumstances," Gates said. "I've worked for eight presidents, and not even Lyndon Johnson or Richard Nixon in their angriest moments would have considered doing or saying some of the things that were said between the election and January 6."

Gates believes that Milley, who served as his military assistant when Gates was Bush's secretary of defense, was uniquely qualified to defend the Constitution from Trump during those final days. "General Milley expected to be fired every single day between Election Day and January 6," he said. A less confident and assertive chairman might not have held the line against Trump's antidemocratic plots.

When I mentioned Gates's assessment to Milley, he demurred. "I think that any of my peers would have done the same thing. Why do I say that? First of all, I know them. Second, we all think the same way about the Constitution."

Some of those who served in Trump's administration say that he appointed Milley chairman because he was drawn to Milley's warrior reputation, tanklike build, and four-star eyebrows. Senator Angus King of Maine, a political independent who is a supporter of Milley's, told me, "Trump picked him as chief because he looks like what Trump thinks a general should look like." But Trump misjudged him, King said. "He thought he would be loyal to him and not to the Constitution." Trump had been led to believe that Milley would be more malleable than other generals. This misunderstanding threatened to become indelibly ingrained in Washington when Milley made what many people consider to be his most serious mistake as chairman. During the George Floyd protests in early June 2020, Milley, wearing combat fatigues, followed Trump out of the White House to Lafayette Square, which had just been cleared of demonstrators by force. Milley realized too late that Trump, who continued across the street to pose for a now-infamous photo while standing in front of a vandalized church, was manipulating him into a visual endorsement of his martial approach to the demonstrations. Though Milley left the entourage before it reached the church, the damage was significant.

A

"We're getting the fuck out of here," Milley said to his security chief. "I'm fucking done with this shit." Esper would later say that he and Milley had been duped.

For Milley, Lafayette Square was an agonizing episode; he described it later as a "road-to-Damascus moment." The week afterward, in a commencement address to the National Defense University, he apologized to the armed forces and the country. "I should not have been there," he said. "My presence in that moment and in that environment created a perception of the military involved in domestic politics." His apology earned him the permanent enmity of Trump, who told him that apologies are a sign of weakness.

Joseph Dunford, the Marine general who preceded Milley as chairman of the Joint Chiefs, had also faced onerous and unusual challenges. But during the first two years of the Trump presidency, Dunford had been supported by officials such as Kelly, Mattis, Tillerson, and McMaster. These men attempted, with intermittent success, to keep the president's most dangerous impulses in check. (According to the Associated Press, Kelly and Mattis made a pact with each other that one of them would remain in the country at all times, so the president would never be left unmonitored.) By the time Milley assumed the chairman's role, all of those officials were gone—driven out or fired.

At the top of the list of worries for these officials was the management of America's nuclear arsenal. Early in Trump's term, when Milley was serving as chief of staff of the Army, Trump entered a cycle of rhetorical warfare with the North Korean dictator Kim Jong Un. At certain points, Trump raised the possibility of attacking North Korea with nuclear weapons, according to *The New York Times* reporter Michael S. Schmidt's book, *Donald Trump v. The United States*. Kelly, Dunford, and others tried to convince Trump that his rhetoric—publicly mocking Kim as "Little Rocket Man," for instance—could trigger nuclear war. "If you keep pushing this clown, he could do something with nuclear weapons," Kelly told him, explaining that Kim, though a dictator, could be pressured by his own military elites to attack American interests in response to Trump's provocations. When that argument failed to work, Kelly spelled out for the president that a nuclear exchange could cost the lives of millions of Koreans and Japanese, as well as those of Americans throughout the Pacific. Guam, Kelly told him, falls within range of North Korean missiles. "Guam isn't America," Trump responded.

Though the specter of a recklessly instigated nuclear confrontation abated when Joe Biden came to office, the threat was still on Milley's mind, which is why he set out to visit Minot that day in March.

In addition to housing the 91st Missile Wing, Minot is home to the Air Force's 5th Bomb Wing, and I watched Milley spend the morning inspecting a fleet of B52 bombers. Milley enjoys meeting the rank and file, and he quizzed

A

air crews—who appeared a little unnerved at being interrogated with such exuberance by the chairman of the Joint Chiefs—about their roles, needs, and responsibilities. We then flew by helicopter to a distant launch-control facility, to visit the missile officers in charge of the Minuteman IIIs. The underground bunker is staffed continuously by two launch officers, who are responsible for a flight of 10 missiles, each secured in hardened underground silos. The two officers seated at the facility's console described to Milley their launch procedures.

The individual silos, connected to the launch-control facility by buried cable, are surrounded by chain-link fences. They are placed at some distance from one another, an arrangement that would force Russia or China to expend a large number of their own missiles to preemptively destroy America's. The silos are also protected by electronic surveillance, and by helicopter and ground patrols. The Hueys carrying us to one of the silos landed well outside the fence, in a farmer's field. Accompanying Milley was Admiral Charles Richard, who was then the commander of Strategic Command, or Stratcom. Stratcom is in charge of America's nuclear force; the commander is the person who would receive orders from the president to launch nuclear weapons—by air, sea, or land—at an adversary.

It was windy and cold at the silo. Air Force officers showed us the 110-ton blast door, and then we walked to an open hatch. Richard mounted a rickety metal ladder leading down into the silo and disappeared from view. Then Milley began his descent. "Just don't touch anything," an Air Force noncommissioned officer said. "Sir."

Then it was my turn. "No smoking down there," the NCO said, helpfully. The ladder dropped 60 feet into a twilight haze, ending at a catwalk that ringed the missile itself. The Minuteman III weighs about 80,000 pounds and is about 60 feet tall. The catwalk surrounded the top of the missile, eye level with its conical warhead. Milley and I stood next to each other, staring silently at the bomb. The warhead of the typical Minuteman III has at least 20 times the explosive power of the bomb that destroyed Hiroshima. We were close enough to touch it, and I, at least, was tempted.

Milley broke the silence. "You ever see one of these before?"

"No," I answered.

"Me neither," Milley said.

I couldn't mask my surprise.

"I'm an infantryman," he said, smiling. "We don't have these in the infantry."

He continued, "I'm testifying in front of Congress on nuclear posture, and I think it's important to see these things for myself."

Richard joined us. "This is an indispensable component of the nuclear triad," he said, beginning a standard Strategic Command pitch. "Our goal is to communicate to potential adversaries: 'Not today.'" (When I later visited Richard at Offutt Air Force Base, the headquarters of Stratcom, near Omaha, Nebraska, I saw that his office features a large sign with this same slogan, hanging above portraits of the leaders of Russia, China, Iran, and North Korea.)

I used this moment in the silo to discuss with Milley the stability of America's nuclear arsenal under Trump. The former president's ignorance of nuclear doctrine had been apparent well before his exchanges with Kim Jong Un. In a 2015 Republican-primary debate, Trump was asked, "Of the three legs of the triad . . . do you have a priority?" Trump's answer: "I think—I think, for me, nuclear is just—the power, the devastation is very important to me." After this, Senator Marco Rubio, a foreign-policy expert who was one of Trump's Republican-primary opponents, called Trump an "erratic individual" who could not be trusted with the country's nuclear codes. (Rubio subsequently embraced Trump, praising him for bringing "a lot of people and energy into the Republican Party.")

I described to Milley a specific worry I'd had, illustrated most vividly by one of the more irrational public statements Trump made as president. On January 2, 2018, Trump tweeted: "North Korean Leader Kim Jong Un just stated that the 'Nuclear Button is on his desk at all times.' Will someone from his depleted and food starved regime please inform him that I too have a Nuclear

Button, but it is a much bigger & more powerful one than his, and my Button works!"

This tweet did not initiate a fatal escalatory cycle, but with it Trump created conditions that easily could have, as he did at several other moments during his presidency. Standing beside the missile in the silo, I expressed my concern about this to Milley.

"Wasn't going to happen," he responded.

"You're not in the chain of command," I noted. The chairman is an adviser to the president, not a field commander.

"True," he answered. "The chain of command runs from the president to the secretary of defense to that guy," he said, pointing to Richard, who had moved to the other side of the catwalk. "We've got excellent professionals throughout the system." He then said, "Nancy Pelosi was worried about this. I told her she didn't have to worry, that we have systems in place." By this, he meant that the system is built to resist the efforts of rogue actors.

Shortly after the assault on the Capitol on January 6, Pelosi, who was then the Speaker of the House, called Milley to ask if the nation's nuclear weapons were secure. "He's crazy," she said of Trump. "You know he's crazy. He's been crazy for a long time. So don't say you don't know what his state of mind is." According to Bob Woodward and Robert Costa, who recounted this conversation in their book, *Peril*, Milley replied, "Madam Speaker, I agree with you on everything." He then said, according to the authors,

"I want you to know this in your heart of hearts, I can guarantee you 110 percent that the military, use of military power, whether it's nuclear or a strike in a foreign country of any kind, we're not going to do anything illegal or crazy."

Shortly after the call from Pelosi, Milley gathered the Pentagon's top nuclear officers—one joined by telephone from Stratcom headquarters—for an emergency meeting. The flag officers in attendance included Admiral Richard; the vice chairman of the Joint Chiefs, General John Hyten, who was Richard's predecessor at Stratcom; and the leaders of the National Military Command Center, the highly secure Pentagon facility from which emergency-action messages—the actual instructions to launch nuclear weapons—would emanate. The center is staffed continuously, and each eight-hour shift conducts drills on nuclear procedures. In the meeting in his office, Milley told the assembled generals and admirals that, out of an abundance of caution, he wanted to go over the procedures and processes for deploying nuclear weapons. Hyten summarized the standard procedures—including ensuring the participation of the Joint Chiefs in any conversation with the president about imminent war. At the conclusion of Hyten's presentation, according to meeting participants, Milley said, "If anything weird or crazy happens, just make sure we all know." Milley then went to each officer in turn and asked if he understood the procedures. They all affirmed that they did. Milley told other members of the Joint Chiefs of Staff, "All we've got to do is see to it that the plane lands on January 20," when the constitutional transfer of power to the new president would be completed.

I found Milley's confidence only somewhat reassuring. The American president is a nuclear monarch, invested with unilateral authority to release weapons that could destroy the planet many times over.

I mentioned to Milley a conversation I'd had with James Mattis when he was the secretary of defense. I had told Mattis, only half-joking, that I was happy he was a physically fit Marine. If it ever came to it, I said, he could forcibly wrest the nuclear football—the briefcase containing, among other things, the authentication codes needed to order a nuclear strike—from the president. Mattis, a wry man, smiled and said that I was failing to take into account the mission of the Secret Service.

When I mentioned to Milley my view that Trump was mentally and morally unequipped to make decisions concerning war and peace, he would say only, "The president alone decides to launch nuclear weapons, but he doesn't launch them alone." He then repeated the sentence.

He has also said in private settings, more colloquially, "The president can't wake up in the middle of the night and decide to push a button. One reason for this is that there's no button to push."

During conversations with Milley and others about the nuclear challenge, a story from the 1970s came frequently

A

to my mind. The story concerns an Air Force officer named Harold Hering, who was dismissed from service for asking a question about a crucial flaw in America's nuclear command-and-control system—a flaw that had no technical solution. Hering was a Vietnam veteran who, in 1973, was training to become a Minuteman crew member. One day in class, he asked, "How can I know that an order I receive to launch my missiles came from a sane president?" The Air Force concluded that launch officers did not need to know the answer to this question, and they discharged him. Hering appealed his discharge, and responded to the Air Force's assertion as follows: "I have to say I feel I do have a need to know, because I am a human being."

The U.S. military possesses procedures and manuals for every possible challenge. Except Hering's.

After we climbed out of the missile silo, I asked Milley how much time the president and the secretary of defense would have to make a decision about using nuclear weapons, in the event of a reported enemy attack. Milley would not answer in specifics, but he acknowledged—as does everyone in the business of thinking about nuclear weapons—that the timeline could be acutely brief. For instance, it is generally believed that if surveillance systems detected an imminent launch from Russia, the president could have as few as five or six minutes to make a decision. "At the highest levels, folks are trained to work through decisions at a rapid clip," Milley said. "These decisions would be very difficult to make. Sometimes the information would be very limited. But we face a lot of hard decisions on a regular basis."

The story of Milley's promotion to the chairmanship captures much about the disorder in Donald Trump's mind, and in his White House.

By 2018, Trump was growing tired of General Dunford, a widely respected Marine officer. After one White House briefing by Dunford, Trump turned to aides and said, "That guy is smart. Why did he join the military?" Trump did not consider Dunford to be sufficiently "loyal," and he was seeking a general who would pledge his personal fealty. Such generals don't tend to exist in the American system—Michael Flynn, Trump's QAnon-addled first national security adviser, is an exception—but Trump was adamant.

The president had also grown tired of James Mattis, the defense secretary. He had hired Mattis in part because he'd been told his nickname was "Mad Dog." It wasn't—that had been a media confection—and Mattis proved far more cerebral, and far more independent-minded, than Trump could handle. So when Mattis recommended David Goldfein, the Air Force chief of staff, to become the next chairman, Trump rejected the choice. (In ordinary presidencies, the defense secretary chooses the chairman of the Joint Chiefs, and the president, by custom, accedes to the choice.)

At that point, Milley was Mattis's choice to serve in a dual-hatted role, as NATO supreme allied commander in

A

Europe and the head of U.S. European Command. Mattis has said he believed Milley's bullish personality made him the perfect person to push America's European allies to spend more on their collective defense, and to focus on the looming threat from Russia.

But a group of ex–Army officers then close to Trump had been lobbying for an Army general for the chairmanship, and Milley, the Army chief of staff, was the obvious candidate. Despite a reputation for being prolix and obstreperous in a military culture that, at its highest reaches, values discretion and rhetorical restraint, Milley was popular with many Army leaders, in part because of the reputation he'd developed in Iraq and Afghanistan as an especially effective war fighter. A son of working-class Boston, Milley is a former hockey player who speaks bluntly, sometimes brutally. "I'm Popeye the fucking sailorman," he has told friends. "I yam what I yam." This group of former Army officers, including Esper, who was then serving as the secretary of the Army, and David Urban, a West Point graduate who was key to Trump's Pennsylvania election effort, believed that Trump would take to Milley, who had both an undergraduate degree from Princeton and the personality of a hockey enforcer. "Knowing Trump, I knew that he was looking for a complete carnivore, and Milley fit that bill," Urban told me. "He checked so many boxes for Trump."

In late 2018, Milley was called to meet the president. Before the meeting, he visited Kelly in his West Wing office, where he was told that Trump might ask him to serve as chairman of the Joint Chiefs. But, if given a choice, Kelly said, he should avoid the role. "If he asks you to go to Europe, you should go. It's crazy here," Kelly said. At the time of this meeting, Kelly was engaged in a series of disputes with Ivanka Trump and Jared Kushner (he referred to them acidly as the "Royal Couple"), and he was having little success imposing order over an administration in chaos. Each day, ex–administration officials told me, aides such as Stephen Miller and Peter Navarro—along with Trump himself—would float absurd, antidemocratic ideas. Dunford had become an expert at making himself scarce in the White House, seeking to avoid these aides and others.

Kelly escorted Milley to the Oval Office. Milley saluted Trump and sat across from the president, who was seated at the Resolute Desk.

"You're here because I'm interviewing you for the job of chairman of the Joint Chiefs of Staff," Trump said. "What do you think of that?"

Milley responded: "I'll do whatever you ask me to do." At which point, Trump turned to Kelly and said, "What's that other job Mattis wants him to do? Something in Europe?"

Kelly answered, "That's SACEUR, the supreme allied commander in Europe."

Trump asked, "What does that guy do?"

"That's the person who commands U.S. forces in Europe," Kelly said.

A

"Which is the better job?" Trump asked.

Kelly answered that the chairmanship is the better job. Trump offered Milley the role. The business of the meeting done, the conversation then veered in many different directions. But at one point Trump returned to the job offer, saying to Milley, "Mattis says you're soft on transgenders. Are you soft on transgenders?"

Milley responded, "I'm not soft on transgender or hard on transgender. I'm about standards in the U.S. military, about who is qualified to serve in the U.S. military. I don't care who you sleep with or what you are."

The offer stood.

It would be nearly a year before Dunford retired and Milley assumed the role. At his welcome ceremony at Joint Base Myer–Henderson Hall, across the Potomac River from the capital, Milley gained an early, and disturbing, insight into Trump's attitude toward soldiers. Milley had chosen a severely wounded Army captain, Luis Avila, to sing "God Bless America." Avila, who had completed five combat tours, had lost a leg in an IED attack in Afghanistan, and had suffered two heart attacks, two strokes, and brain damage as a result of his injuries. To Milley, and to four-star generals across the Army, Avila and his wife, Claudia, represented the heroism, sacrifice, and dignity of wounded soldiers.

It had rained that day, and the ground was soft; at one point Avila's wheelchair threatened to topple over. Milley's wife, Hollyanne, ran to help Avila, as did Vice President Mike Pence. After Avila's performance, Trump walked over to congratulate him, but then said to Milley, within earshot of several witnesses, "Why do you bring people like that here? No one wants to see that, the wounded." Never let Avila appear in public again, Trump told Milley. (Recently, Milley invited Avila to sing at his retirement ceremony.)

These sorts of moments, which would grow in intensity and velocity, were disturbing to Milley. As a veteran of multiple combat tours in Iraq and Afghanistan, he had buried 242 soldiers who'd served under his command. Milley's family venerated the military, and Trump's attitude toward the uniformed services seemed superficial, callous, and, at the deepest human level, repugnant.

Milley was raised in a blue-collar section of Winchester, Massachusetts, just outside Boston, where nearly everyone of a certain age—including his mother—was a World War II veteran. Mary Murphy served in the women's branch of the Naval Reserve; the man who became her husband, Alexander Milley, was a Navy corpsman who was part of the assault landings in the central Pacific at Kwajalein, Tinian, and Iwo Jima. Alexander was just out of high school when he enlisted. "My dad brought his hockey skates to the Pacific," Milley told me. "He was pretty naive."

Though he was born after it ended, World War II made a powerful impression on Mark Milley, in part because it

A

had imprinted itself so permanently on his father. When I traveled to Japan with Milley this summer, he told me a story about the stress his father had experienced during his service. Milley was undergoing a bit of stress himself on this trip. He was impeccably diplomatic with his Japanese counterparts, but I got the impression that he still finds visiting the country to be slightly surreal. At one point he was given a major award in the name of the emperor. "If my father could only see this," he said to me, and then recounted the story.

It took place at Fort Drum, in upstate New York, when Milley was taking command of the 10th Mountain Division, in 2011. His father and his father's younger brother Tom, a Korean War veteran, came to attend his change-of-command ceremony. "My father always hated officers," Milley recalled. "Every day from the time I was a second lieutenant to colonel, he was like, 'When are you getting out?' Then, all of sudden, it was 'My son, the general.'"

He continued, "We have the whole thing—troops on the field, regalia, cannons, bugle—and then we have a reception back at the house. I've got the Japanese flag up on the wall, right over the fireplace. It's a flag my father took from Saipan. So that night, he's sitting there in his T-shirt and boxers; he's having probably more than one drink, just staring at the Japanese flag. One or two in the morning, we hear this primeval-type screaming. He's screaming at his brother, 'Tom, you got to get up!' And I'll say it the way he said it: 'Tom, the Japs are here, the Japs are here! We gotta get the kids outta here!' So my wife elbows me and says, 'Your father,' and I say, 'Yes, I figured that out,' and I go out and my dad, he's not in good shape by then—in his 80s, Parkinson's, not super mobile—and yet he's running down the hallway. I grab him by both arms. His eyes are bugging out and I say, 'Dad, it's okay, you're with the 10th Mountain Division on the Canadian border.' And his brother Tom comes out and says, 'Goddamnit, just go to fucking bed, for Chrissakes. You won your war; we just tied ours.' And I feel like I'm in some B movie. Anyway, he calmed down, but you see, this is what happens. One hundred percent of people who see significant combat have some form of PTSD. For years he wouldn't go to the VA, and I finally said, 'You hit the beach at Iwo Jima and Saipan. The VA is there for you; you might as well use it.' And they diagnosed him, finally."

Milley never doubted that he would follow his parents into military service, though he had no plans to make the Army a career. At Princeton, which recruited him to play hockey, he was a political-science major, writing his senior thesis on Irish revolutionary guerrilla movements. He joined ROTC, and he was commissioned as a second lieutenant in June 1980. He began his Army career as maintenance officer in a motor pool of the 82nd Airborne; this did not excite

A

him, so he maneuvered his way onto a path that took him to the Green Berets.

His first overseas mission was to parachute into Somalia in 1984 with a five-man Special Forces A-Team to train a Somali army detachment that was fighting Soviet-backed Ethiopia. "It was basically dysentery and worms," he recalled. "We were out there in the middle of nowhere. It was all small-unit tactics, individual skills. We were boiling water we got from cow ponds, and breakfast was an ostrich egg and flatbread." His abiding interest in insurgencies led him to consider a career in the CIA, but he was dissuaded by a recruiter who told him working in the agency would make having any kind of family life hard. In 1985, he was sent to Fort Ord, where he "got really excited about the Army." This was during the Reagan-era defense buildup, when the Army—now all-volunteer—was emerging from what Milley describes as its "post-Vietnam malaise." This was a time of war-fighting innovation, which Milley would champion as he rose in rank. He would go on to take part in the invasion of Panama, and he helped coordinate the occupation of northern Haiti during the U.S. intervention there in 1994.

After September 11, 2001, Milley deployed repeatedly as a brigade commander to Iraq and Afghanistan. Ross Davidson, a retired colonel who served as Milley's operations officer in Baghdad when he commanded a brigade of the 10th Mountain Division, recalled Milley's mantra:

"Move to the sound of the guns." Davidson went on to say, with admiration, "I've been blown up, like, nine times with the guy."

Davidson witnessed what is often mentioned as Milley's most notable act of personal bravery, when he ran across a booby-trapped bridge at night to stop a pair of U.S. tanks from crossing. "We had no communication with the tanks, and the boss just ran across the bridge without thinking of his own safety to keep those tanks from blowing themselves up," he told me. "It was something to see."

Davidson and others who fought for Milley remember him as ceaselessly aggressive. "We're rolling down a street and we knew we were going to get hit—the street just went deserted—and *bam, smack*, a round explodes to our right," Davidson said. "Everything goes black, the windshield splinters in front of us, one of our gunners took a chunk of shrapnel. We bailed out and Milley says, 'Oh, you want a fight? Let's fight.' We started hunting down bad guys. Milley sends one Humvee back with the wounded, and then we're kicking doors down." At another point, Davidson said, "he wanted to start a fight in this particular area north of the city, farm fields mixed with little hamlets. And so we moved to the middle of this field, just circled the wagons and waited to draw fire. He was brought up in a school of thought that says a commander who conducts command-and-control from a fixed command post is isolated in many regards. He was in the battle space almost every day."

A

Once, when the commanding general of the 10th Mountain Division, Lloyd Austin—now the secretary of defense—was visiting Baghdad, Milley took him on a tour of the city. Milley, Austin, and Davidson were in a Humvee when it was hit.

"Mark has the gift of gab. I don't remember what he was talking about, but he was talking when there was an explosion. Our second vehicle got hit. Austin's window shattered, but we didn't stop; we punched through," Davidson said. "Wedged into Austin's door was this four-inch chunk of shrapnel. If it had breached the door seam, it would have taken Austin's head clean off. It was a 'Holy shit, we almost got the commanding general killed' type of situation. That wouldn't have gone well."

(When I mentioned this incident recently to Austin, he said, "I thought that was Mark trying to kill his boss." That's an elaborate way to kill the boss, I said. "You've got to make it look credible," Austin answered, smiling.)

Dunford, Milley's predecessor as chairman of the Joint Chiefs, was the four-star commander of NATO forces in Afghanistan in 2013 when Milley, by then a three-star general, came to serve as the international joint commander of all ground forces in the country. He describes Milley as ambitious and creative. "He was very forward-leaning, and he set the bar very high for himself and others," Dunford told me. "He puts a lot of pressure on himself to perform. There's just a level of ambition and aggressiveness there. It would be hard for me to imagine that someone could have accomplished as much as he did in the role. Hockey was the right sport for him."

Soon after becoming chairman, Milley found himself in a disconcerting situation: trying, and failing, to teach President Trump the difference between appropriate battlefield aggressiveness on the one hand, and war crimes on the other. In November 2019, Trump decided to intervene in three different cases that had been working their way through the military justice system. In the most infamous case, the Navy SEAL Eddie Gallagher had been found guilty of posing with the corpse of an Islamic State prisoner. Though Gallagher was found not guilty of murder, witnesses testified that he'd stabbed the prisoner in the neck with a hunting knife. (Gallagher's nickname was "Blade.") In an extraordinary move, Trump reversed the Navy's decision to demote him in rank. Trump also pardoned a junior Army officer, Clint Lorance, convicted of second-degree murder for ordering soldiers to shoot three unarmed Afghans, two of whom died. In the third case, a Green Beret named Mathew Golsteyn was accused of killing an unarmed Afghan he suspected was a bomb maker for the Taliban and then covering up the killing. At a rally in Florida that month, Trump boasted, "I stuck up for three great warriors against the deep state."

The president's intervention included a decision that Gallagher should be allowed to keep his Trident insignia, which is worn by all SEALs in good standing. The pin features an anchor and an eagle holding a flintlock pistol while sitting atop a horizontal trident. It is one of the most coveted insignia in the entire U.S. military.

This particular intervention was onerous for the Navy, because by tradition only a commanding officer or a group of SEALs on a Trident Review Board are meant to decide if one of their own is unworthy of being a SEAL. Late one night, on Air Force One, Milley tried to convince Trump that his intrusion was damaging Navy morale. They were flying from Washington to Dover Air Force Base, in Delaware, to attend a "dignified transfer," the repatriation ceremony for fallen service members.

"Mr. President," Milley said, "you have to understand that the SEALs are a tribe within a larger tribe, the Navy. And it's up to them to figure out what to do with Gallagher. You don't want to intervene. This is up to the tribe. They have their own rules that they follow."

Trump called Gallagher a hero and said he didn't understand why he was being punished.

"Because he slit the throat of a wounded prisoner," Milley said.

"The guy was going to die anyway," Trump said.

Milley answered, "Mr. President, we have military ethics and laws about what happens in battle. We can't do that kind of thing. It's a war crime." Trump answered that he didn't understand "the big deal." He went on, "You guys"—meaning combat soldiers—"are all just killers. What's the difference?"

At which point a frustrated Milley summoned one of his aides, a combat-veteran SEAL officer, to the president's Air Force One office. Milley took hold of the Trident pin on the SEAL's chest and asked him to describe its importance. The aide explained to Trump that, by tradition, only SEALs can decide, based on assessments of competence and character, whether one of their own should lose his pin. But the president's mind was not changed. Gallagher kept his pin.

When I asked Milley about these incidents, he explained his larger views about behavior in combat. "You have accidents that occur, and innocent people get killed in warfare," he said. "Then you have the intentional breaking of the rules of war that occurs in part because of the psychological and moral degradation that occurs to all human beings who participate in combat. It takes an awful lot of moral and physical discipline to prevent you or your unit from going down that path of degradation.

"I'll use Gallagher as an example. He's a tough guy, a tough, hard Navy SEAL. Saw a lot of combat. There's a little bit of a 'There but for the grace of God go I' feeling in all of this. What happened to Gallagher can happen to many human beings." Milley told me about a book given to him by a friend, Aviv Kochavi, a former chief of staff of the Israel Defense Forces. The book, by an American academic named

Christopher Browning, is called *Ordinary Men: Reserve Police Battalion 101 and the Final Solution in Poland*.

"It's a great book," Milley said. "It's about these average police officers from Hamburg who get drafted, become a police battalion that follows the Wehrmacht into Poland, and wind up slaughtering Jews and committing genocide. They just devolve into barbaric acts. It's about moral degradation."

During Milley's time in the Trump administration, the disagreements and misunderstandings between the Pentagon and the White House all seemed to follow the same pattern: The president—who was incapable of understanding or unwilling to understand the aspirations and rules that guide the military—would continually try to politicize an apolitical institution. This conflict reached its nadir with the Lafayette Square incident in June 2020. The day when Milley appeared in uniform by the president's side, heading into the square, has been studied endlessly. What is clear is that Milley (and Mark Esper) walked into an ambush, and Milley extracted himself as soon as he could, which was too late.

The image of a general in combat fatigues walking with a president who has a well-known affection for the Insurrection Act—the 1807 law that allows presidents to deploy the military to put down domestic riots and rebellions—caused consternation and anger across the senior-officer ranks, and among retired military leaders.

"I absolutely, positively shouldn't have been there," Milley says of Lafayette Square. "I'm a soldier, and fundamental to this republic is for the military to stay out of politics."

"I just about ended my friendship with Mark over Lafayette Square," General Peter Chiarelli, the now-retired former vice chief of staff of the Army, told me. Chiarelli was once Milley's superior, and he considered him to be among his closest friends. "I watched him in uniform, watched the whole thing play out, and I was pissed. I wrote an editorial about the proper role of the military that was very critical of Mark, and I was about to send it, and my wife said, 'You really want to do that—end a treasured friendship—like this?' She said I should send it to him instead, and of course she was right." When they spoke, Milley made no excuses, but said it had not been his intention to look as if he was doing Trump's bidding. Milley explained the events of the day to Chiarelli: He was at FBI headquarters, and had been planning to visit National Guardsmen stationed near the White House when he was summoned to the Oval Office. Once he arrived, Trump signaled to everyone present that they were heading outside. Ivanka Trump found a Bible and they were on their way.

"As a commissioned officer, I have a duty to ensure that the military stays out of politics," Milley told me. "This was a political act, a political event. I didn't realize it at the moment. I probably should have, but I didn't, until the event was well on its way. I peeled off before the church, but we're already a minute or two into this thing, and it was clear to me that it was a political event, and I was in uniform. I absolutely, positively shouldn't have been there. The political people, the president and others, can do whatever they want. But I can't. I'm a soldier, and fundamental to this republic is for the military to stay out of politics."

Trump, inflamed by the sight of protesters so close to the White House, had been behaving especially erratically. "You are losers!" the president screamed at Cabinet members and other top officials at one point. "You are all fucking losers!"

According to Esper, Trump desperately wanted a violent response to the protesters, asking, "Can't you just shoot them? Just shoot them in the legs or something?" When I raised this with Milley, he explained, somewhat obliquely, how he would manage the president's eruptions.

"It was a rhetorical question," Milley explained. "'Can't you just shoot them in the legs?'"

"He never actually ordered you to shoot anyone in the legs?" I asked.

"Right. This could be interpreted many, many different ways," he said.

Milley and others around Trump used different methods to handle the unstable president. "You can judge my success or failure on this, but I always tried to use persuasion with the president, not undermine or go around him or slow-roll," Milley told me. "I would present my argument to him. The president makes decisions, and if the president ordered us to do X, Y, or Z and it was legal, we would do it. If it's not legal, it's my job to say it's illegal, and here's why it's illegal. I would emphasize cost and risk of the various courses of action. My job, then and now, is to let the president know what the course of action could be, let them know what the cost is, what the risks and benefits are. And then make a recommendation. That's what I've done under both presidents."

He went on to say, "President Trump never ordered me to tell the military to do something illegal. He never did that. I think that's an important point."

We were discussing the Lafayette Square incident while at Quarters Six, the chairman's home on Generals' Row at Fort Myer, in Arlington, Virginia, across the Potomac from the Washington Monument, the Lincoln Memorial, and the Capitol. Next door to Quarters Six was the home of the Air Force chief of staff, General Charles Q. Brown Jr., who is slated to become the next chairman. Generals' Row was built on land seized by the Union from Robert E. Lee's plantation. It is a good place to hold a discussion about the relationship between a democracy and its standing army.

I tried to ask Milley why Lafayette Square had caught him off guard, given all that he had seen and learned already. Only a few weeks earlier, Trump had declared to the Joint Chiefs of Staff, in a meeting about China, that the "great U.S. military isn't as capable as you think." After the meeting, Milley spoke with the chiefs, who were angry and flustered by the president's behavior. (Esper writes in his memoir, *A Sacred Oath*, that one member of the Joint Chiefs began studying the Twenty-Fifth Amendment, which can be used to remove an unfit president.)

"Weren't you aware that Trump—"

"I wasn't aware that this was going to be a political event."

I tacked. "Were you aware that this was"—I paused, searching for an artful term—"an unusual administration?"

"I'll reserve comment on that," Milley responded. "I think there were certainly plenty of warnings and indicators that others might say in hindsight were there. But for me, I'm a soldier, and my task is to follow lawful orders and maintain good order and discipline in the force."

"You didn't have situational awareness?"

"At that moment, I didn't realize that there was a highly charged piece of political stagecraft going on, if you will. And when I did, I peeled off." (That evening, Lieutenant General McMaster texted Milley the well-known meme of Homer Simpson disappearing into a hedge.)

The lesson, Milley said, was that he had to pay more attention. "I had to double down on ensuring that I personally—and that the uniformed military—that we all stayed clear of any political acts or anything that could be implied as being involved in politics."

The week after Lafayette Square, Milley made his apology in the National Defense University speech—a speech that helped repair his relationship with the officer corps but destroyed his relationship with Trump.

"There are different gradients of what is bad. The really bad days are when people get killed in combat," Milley told me. "But those 90 seconds were clearly a low point from a personal and professional standpoint for me, over the course of 43, 44 years of service. They were searing. It was a bad moment for me because it struck at the heart of the credibility of the institution."

The chasm dividing Milley and Trump on matters of personal honor became obvious after Lafayette Square. In a statement, referring to Milley's apology, Trump said of the chairman, "I saw at that moment he had no courage or skill."

Milley viewed it differently. "Apologies are demonstrations of strength," Milley told me. "There's a whole concept of redemption in Western philosophy. It's part and parcel of our philosophy, the Western religious tradition—the idea that human beings are fallible, that we sin and that we make mistakes and that when you do so you own the mistake, you admit it, and then you learn from that mistake and take corrective action and move on."

For his part, General Chiarelli concluded that his friend had simply been in the wrong place at the wrong time.

A

Quoting Peter Feaver, an academic expert on civil-military relations, Chiarelli said, "You have to judge Mark like you judge Olympic divers—by the difficulty of the dive."

That summer, Milley visited Chiarelli in Washington State and, over breakfast, described what he thought was coming next. "It was unbelievable. This is August 2, and he laid out in specific detail what his concerns were between August and Inauguration Day. He identified one of his biggest concerns as January 6," the day the Senate was to meet to certify the election. "It was almost like a crystal ball."

Chiarelli said that Milley told him it was possible, based on his observations of the president and his advisers, that they would not accept an Election Day loss. Specifically, Milley worried that Trump would trigger a war—an "October surprise"—to create chaotic conditions in the lead-up to the election. Chiarelli mentioned the continuous skirmishes inside the White House between those who were seeking to attack Iran, ostensibly over its nuclear program, and those, like Milley, who could not justify a large-scale preemptive strike.

In the crucial period after his road-to-Damascus conversion, Milley set several goals for himself: keep the U.S. out of reckless, unnecessary wars overseas; maintain the military's integrity, and his own; and prevent the administration from using the military against the American people. He told uniformed and civilian officials that the military would play no part in any attempt by Trump to illegally remain in office.

The desire on the part of Trump and his loyalists to utilize the Insurrection Act was unabating. Stephen Miller, the Trump adviser whom Milley is said to have called "Rasputin," was vociferous on this point. Less than a week after George Floyd was murdered, Miller told Trump in an Oval Office meeting, "Mr. President, they are burning America down. Antifa, Black Lives Matter—they're burning it down. You have an insurrection on your hands. Barbarians are at the gate."

According to Woodward and Costa in *Peril*, Milley responded, "Shut the fuck up, Steve." Then he turned to Trump. "Mr. President, they are not burning it down."

I asked Milley to describe the evolution of his post–Lafayette Square outlook. "You know this term *teachable moment*?" he asked. "Every month thereafter I just did something publicly to continually remind the force about our responsibilities . . . What I'm trying to do the entire summer, all the way up to today, is keep the military out of actual politics."

He continued, "We stay out of domestic politics, period, full stop, not authorized, not permitted, illegal, immoral, unethical—we don't do it." I asked if he ever worried about pockets of insurrectionists within the military.

"We're a very large organization—2.1 million people, active duty and reserves. Some of the people in the

A

organization get outside the bounds of the law. We have that on occasion. We're a highly disciplined force dedicated to the protection of the Constitution and the American people . . . Are there one or two out there who have other thoughts in their mind? Maybe. But the system of discipline works."

"So you had no anxiety at all?"

"Of anything large-scale? Not at all. Not then, not now."

In the weeks before the election, Milley was a dervish of activity. He spent much of his time talking with American allies and adversaries, all worried about the stability of the United States. In what would become his most discussed move, first reported by Woodward and Costa, he called Chinese general Li Zuocheng, his People's Liberation Army counterpart, on October 30, after receiving intelligence that China believed Trump was going to order an attack. "General Li, I want to assure you that the American government is stable and everything is going to be okay," Milley said, according to *Peril*. "We are not going to attack or conduct any kinetic operations against you. General Li, you and I have known each other for now five years. If we're going to attack, I'm going to call you ahead of time. It's not going to be a surprise . . . If there was a war or some kind of kinetic action between the United States and China, there's going to be a buildup, just like there has been always in history."

Milley later told the Senate Armed Services Committee that this call, and a second one two days after the January 6 insurrection, represented an attempt to "deconflict military actions, manage crisis, and prevent war between great powers that are armed with the world's most deadliest weapons."

The October call was endorsed by Secretary of Defense Esper, who was just days away from being fired by Trump. Esper's successor, Christopher Miller, had been informed of the January call. Listening in on the calls were at least 10 U.S. officials, including representatives of the State Department and the CIA. This did not prevent Trump partisans, and Trump himself, from calling Milley "treasonous" for making the calls. (When news of the calls emerged, Miller condemned Milley for them—even though he later conceded that he'd been aware of the second one.)

Milley also spoke with lawmakers and media figures in the days leading up to the election, promising that the military would play no role in its outcome. In a call on the Saturday before Election Day, Milley told news anchors including George Stephanopoulos, Lester Holt, and Norah O'Donnell that the military's role was to protect democracy, not undermine it. "The context was 'We know how fraught things are, and we have a sense of what might happen, and we're not going to let Trump do it,'" Stephanopoulos told me. "He was saying that the military was there to serve the country, and it was clear by implication that the military was not going to be part of a coup." It seemed, Stephanopoulos said, that Milley was "desperately trying not to politicize the military."

When the election arrived, Milley's fear—that the president would not accept the outcome—came to pass. A few days later, when Acting Secretary Miller arrived at the Pentagon accompanied by a coterie of fellow Trump loyalists, including Kash Patel, senior officers in the building were unnerved. Patel has stated his conviction that the Pentagon is riddled with "deep state" operatives.

A few days after Esper's firing, Milley gave a Veterans Day speech, in the presence of Miller, to remind the armed forces—and those who would manipulate them—of their oath to the Constitution. The speech was delivered at the opening of the National Army Museum at Fort Belvoir, in Virginia.

"The motto of the United States Army for over 200 years, since 14 June 1775 . . . has been 'This we will defend,'" Milley said. "And the 'this' refers to the Constitution and to protect the liberty of the American people. You see, we are unique among armies. We are unique among militaries. We do not take an oath to a king or queen, a tyrant or dictator. We do not take an oath to an individual. No, we do not take an oath to a country, a tribe, or religion. We take an oath to the Constitution . . . We will never turn our back on our duty to protect and defend the idea that is America, the Constitution of the United States, against all enemies, foreign and domestic."

He closed with words from Thomas Paine: "These are times that try men's souls. And the summer soldier and the sunshine Patriot will in this crisis shrink from the service of their country. But he who stands by it deserves the love of man and woman. For tyranny, like hell, is not easily conquered."

When Miller followed Milley, his remarks betrayed a certain level of obliviousness; Milley's speech had sounded like a warning shot directed squarely at hard-core Trumpists like him. "Chairman, thanks for setting the bar very high for the new guy to come in and make a few words," Miller said. "I think all I would say to your statements is 'Amen.' Well done."

I asked Milley later if he'd had Miller in mind when he gave that speech.

"Not at all," he said. "My audience was those in uniform. At this point, we are six days or so after the election. It was already contested, already controversial—and I wanted to remind the uniformed military that our oath is to the Constitution and that we have no role to play in politics."

He would remain a dervish until Inauguration Day: reassuring allies and cautioning adversaries; arguing against escalation with Iran; reminding the Joint Chiefs and the National Military Command Center to be aware of unusual requests or demands; and keeping an eye on the activities of the men dispatched by Trump to lead the Pentagon after Esper was fired, men who Milley and others suspected were interested in using the military to advance Trump's efforts to remain president.

Shortly after Esper was fired, Milley told both Patel and Ezra Cohen-Watnick, another Trump loyalist sent to the Pentagon, that he would make sure they would see the world "from behind bars" if they did anything illegal to prevent Joe Biden from taking the oath of office on January 20. (Both men have denied being warned in this manner.)

I asked Milley recently about his encounters with Trump's men. As is his on-the-record custom, he minimized the drama of those days.

I said, "You literally warned political appointees that they would be punished if they engaged in treasonous activities."

He responded: "I didn't do that. Someone saying I did that?"

"You warned Kash Patel and others that they were fucking around and shouldn't have been."

"I didn't warn anybody that I would hold them accountable for anything."

"You warned them that they would be held accountable for breaking the law or violating their oaths."

Suddenly, acquiescence.

"Yeah, sure, in conversation," he said. "It's my job to give advice, so I was advising people that we must follow the law. I give advice all the time."

Today Milley says, about Trump and his closest advisers, "I'm not going to say whether I thought there was a civilian coup or not. I'm going to leave that to the American people to determine, and a court of law, and you're seeing that play out every day. All I'm saying is that my duty as the senior officer of the United States military is to keep out of politics."

What is certain is that, when January 20 finally arrived, Milley exhaled. According to *I Alone Can Fix It*, by *The Washington Post* reporters Carol Leonnig and Philip Rucker, when Michelle Obama asked Milley at the inauguration how he was doing, he replied: "No one has a bigger smile today than I do."

The arrival of a new president did not mean an end to challenges for Milley, or the Pentagon. Attempts to enlist the military in America's zero-sum culture war only intensified. Elements of the hard right, for instance, would exploit manifestations of performative leftism—a drag show on an Air Force base, for instance—to argue that the military under Biden was hopelessly weak and "woke." (Never mind that this was the same military that Trump, while president, had declared the strongest in history.) And in an unprecedented act of interference in the normal functioning of the military, Republican senator Tommy Tuberville of Alabama has placed holds on the promotions of hundreds of senior officers to protest the Defense Department's abortion policies. The officers affected by the Tuberville holds do not make such policies.

An even more substantial blow to morale and force cohesion came late in the summer of 2021, when American forces were withdrawn from Afghanistan against the advice of Milley and most other senior military leaders. The withdrawal—originally proposed by Trump, but ordered by Biden—was criticized by many veterans and active-duty soldiers, and the damage was exacerbated by the callous manner in which Biden treated America's Afghan allies.

This summer, Milley and I visited the War Memorial of Korea, in Seoul, where Milley laid a wreath in front of a wall containing the names of hundreds of Massachusetts men killed in that war. I asked him about the end of America's war in Afghanistan.

"I've got three tours in Afghanistan," he said. "I lost a lot of soldiers in Afghanistan, and for any of us who served there and saw a considerable amount of combat in Afghanistan, that war did not end the way any of us wanted it to end."

"Do you consider it a loss?"

"I think it was a strategic failure," he answered, refusing to repeat the word I used. "When the enemy you've been fighting for 20 years captures the capital and unseats the government you're supporting, that cannot be called anything else."

He continued, "We sunk a tremendous amount of resources, a tremendous amount of money, and, most importantly, lives into helping the Afghan people and giving them hope for a better future. For 20 years we did that. And our primary goal for going there was to prevent al-Qaeda or any other terrorist organization from striking the United States ever again. That was the strategic promise President Bush made to the American people. And we have not, to date, been attacked from Afghanistan, so all the soldiers, sailors, airmen, and Marines that served in Afghanistan should hold their heads high and should be proud of their contributions to American national security. But at the end of the day, the Taliban took the capital."

Milley had recommended to Biden that the U.S. maintain a residual force of soldiers to buttress the American-allied government in Kabul. Biden, Milley said, listened to the military's advice, weighed it, and then chose another path. "It was a lawful order, and we carried out a lawful order," Milley said.

But, I asked him, did he think Afghanistan was winnable?

"I think it would have been a sustainable level of effort over time," he answered. "Take where we're at right now. We are still in Korea today, 70 years after the armistice

A

was signed. When North Korea came across the border in the summer of 1950, the South Korean military was essentially a constabulary, and we had a limited number of advisers here. And then we reinforced very rapidly from our occupation forces in Japan, and then we fought the Korean War. So we ended up preventing North Korea from conquering South Korea, and that effort led to one of the most flourishing countries in the world."

He went on to say, however, that he understood why leaders of both political parties, and a majority of Americans, wanted U.S. troops pulled out of Afghanistan. "These operations aren't sustainable without the will of the people," he said. "Would I and every soldier who served there wish that there was a better outcome? Absolutely, yes, and to that extent, that's a regret.

"The end in Afghanistan didn't happen because of a couple of decisions in the last days," he said. "It was cumulative decisions over 20 years. The American people, as expressed in various polls, and two presidents of two different parties and the majority of members of Congress wanted us to withdraw—and we did."

If the withdrawal from Afghanistan was a low, then a continuing high point for the Defense Department is its enormous effort to keep the Ukrainian army in the fight against Russia. Milley and Lloyd Austin, his former commander and Biden's secretary of defense, have created a useful partnership, particularly regarding Ukraine.

The two men could not be more unalike: Milley cannot stop talking, and Austin is loath to speak more than the minimum number of words necessary to get through the day. But they seem to trust each other, and they sought, after Austin's appointment, to bring stability back to the Pentagon. When I met Austin in his office in mid-September, he alluded to this common desire, and to the turbulence of the recent past. "We needed to make sure we had the relationship right and the swim lanes right— who is responsible for what," he said. "The trust was there, so it was easy to work together to reestablish what we both knew should be the rules of the road."

The massive effort to equip, train, and provide intelligence to Ukrainian forces—all while preventing the outbreak of direct warfare between the U.S. and Russia—must be considered (provisionally, of course) a consequential achievement of the Austin-Milley team. "We've provided Ukraine with its best chance of success in protecting its sovereign territory," Austin told me. "We've pulled NATO together in a way that's not been done, ever. This requires a lot of work by the Department of Defense. If you look at what he and I do every month—we're talking with ministers of defense and chiefs of defense every month—it's extraordinary."

Milley has been less hawkish than some Biden-administration officials on the war with Russia. But he agrees that Ukraine is now the main battlefield between authoritarianism and the democratic order.

A

"World War II ended with the establishment of the rules-based international order. People often ridicule it—they call it 'globalism' and so on—but in fact, in my view, World War II was fought in order to establish a better peace," Milley told me. "We the Americans are the primary authors of the basic rules of the road—and these rules are under stress, and they're fraying at the edges. That's why Ukraine is so important. President Putin has made a mockery of those rules. He's making a mockery of everything. He has assaulted the very first principle of the United Nations, which is that you can't tolerate wars of aggression and you can't allow large countries to attack small countries by military means. He is making a direct frontal assault on the rules that were written in 1945."

The magnitude of this assault requires a commensurate response, but with a vigilant eye toward the worst possible outcome, nuclear war. "It is incumbent upon all of us in positions of leadership to do the very best to maintain a sense of global stability," Milley told me. "If we don't, we're going to pay the butcher's bill. It will be horrific, worse than World War I, worse than World War II."

The close relationship between Milley and Austin may help explain one of Milley's missteps as chairman: his congressional testimony on the subject of critical race theory and "white rage." In June 2021, both Milley and Austin were testifying before the House Armed Services Committee when Michael Waltz, a Republican representative from Florida (and, like Milley, a former Green Beret), asked Austin about a lecture given at West Point called "Understanding Whiteness and White Rage." Austin said that the lecture sounded to him like "something that should not occur." A short while later, Milley provided his own, more expansive views. "I want to understand white rage, and I'm white," he said. And then it seemed as if the anger he felt about the assault on the Capitol spilled out of its container. "What is it that caused thousands of people to assault this building and try to overturn the Constitution of the United States of America?" he asked. "What is wrong with having some situational understanding about the country for which we are here to defend?"

These comments caused a new round of criticism of Milley in some senior military circles, including from generals who agreed with him but believed that this sort of commentary was the purview of the political echelon.

Colonel Ross Davidson, Milley's former operations officer, who was watching the hearing, told me he thinks Milley's contempt for the January 6 insurrectionists was not the only thing that motivated his testimony. Seeing Austin, the first Black secretary of defense and his friend, under sustained criticism led Milley, as Davidson describes it, to "move to the sound of the guns."

"That's in his nature," Davidson said. "'Hey, man, my battle buddy Lloyd is being attacked.'"

Today, Austin defends Milley's statements: "In one instance, in one academic institution, a professor was exposing his students to this," he said, referring to critical race theory. "If you are familiar with all of our curriculum and what we do in our various schools and how we train leaders, it's kind of upsetting and insulting" to suggest that the military has gone "woke."

When I asked Milley recently about this episode, his answer was, predictably, lengthier, more caustic, and substantially more fervent.

"There's a lot of discourse around whether it's a tough Army or a woke Army," he said, referring to commentary on right-wing news channels. "Here's my answer: First of all, it's all bullshit. Second, these accusations are coming from people who don't know what they're talking about. They're doing it for political purposes. Our military wasn't woke 24 months ago, and now it's woke?"

He continued, "You want woke? I'll give you woke. Here's what your military's doing: There are 5,000 sorties a day, including combat patrols protecting the U.S.A. and our interests around the world. At least 60 to 100 Navy warships are patrolling the seven seas, keeping the world free for ocean transport. We have 250,000 troops overseas, in 140 countries, defending the rules-based international order. We've got kids training constantly. This military is trained, well equipped, well led, and focused on readiness. Our readiness statuses are at the highest levels they've been in 20 years. So this idea of a woke military is total, utter, made-up bullshit. They are taking two or three incidents, single anecdotes, a drag show that is against DOD policy. I don't think these shows should be on bases, and neither does the secretary of defense or the chain of command."

This table-pounder of a speech prompted an obvious question: What will Milley say publicly once he's retired? Donald Trump is the presumptive favorite to win the Republican nomination for president, and Trump represents to Milley—as numerous books, and my understanding of the man, strongly suggest—an existential threat to American democracy.

"I won't speak up in politics. I won't. You can hold me to it," he said. "I'm not going to comment on elected officials. I'll comment on policies, which is my purview. I have a certain degree of expertise and experience that I think enable me to make rational contributions to conversations about complex topics about war and peace. To make personal comments on certain political leaders, I don't think that's my place."

Never?

"There are exceptions that can be made under certain circumstances," he said. "But they're pretty rare."

It is hard to imagine Milley restraining himself if Trump attacks him directly—and it is as close to a sure thing as you can have in American politics that Trump will. At one point during his presidency, Trump proposed calling back to active duty two retired flag officers who had been critical of him, Admiral William McRaven and General Stanley McChrystal, so that they could be court-martialed. Mark Esper, who was the defense secretary at the time, says he and Milley had to talk Trump out of such a plan.

During one conversation at Quarters Six, Milley said, "If there's something we've learned from history, it's that aggression left unanswered leads to more aggression." He was talking about Vladimir Putin, but I got the sense that he was talking about someone else as well.

If Trump is reelected president, there will be no Espers or Milleys in his administration. Nor will there be any officials of the stature and independence of John Kelly, H. R. McMaster, or James Mattis. Trump and his allies have already threatened officials they see as disloyal with imprisonment, and there is little reason to imagine that he would not attempt to carry out his threats.

Milley has told friends that he expects that if Trump returns to the White House, the newly elected president will come after him. "He'll start throwing people in jail, and I'd be on the top of the list," he has said. But he's also told friends that he does not believe the country will reelect Trump.

When I asked him about this, he wouldn't answer directly, but when I asked him to describe his level of optimism about the country's future, he said: "I have a lot of confidence in the general officer corps, and I have confidence in the American people. The United States of America is an extraordinarily resilient country, agile and flexible, and the inherent goodness of the American people is there. I've always believed that, and I will go to my grave believing that."

I pressed him: "After all you've been through, you believe that?"

"There are bumps in the road, to be sure, and you get through the bumps, but I don't want to overstate this. What did I do? All I did was try to preserve the integrity of the military and to keep the military out of domestic politics. That's all I did."

These assertions will be debated for a long time. But it is fair to say that Milley came close to red lines that are meant to keep uniformed officers from participating in politics. It is also fair to say that no president has ever challenged the idea of competent civilian control in the manner of Donald Trump, and that no president has ever threatened the constitutional underpinnings of the American project in the manner Trump has. The apportionment of responsibility in the American system—presidents give orders; the military carries them out—works best when the president is sane. The preservation of a proper civil-military relationship is hugely important to democracy—but so, too, is universal acceptance of the principle that political officials leave office when they lose legitimate elections.

A

As Milley cedes the chairmanship, he also cedes Quarters Six. I visited him there on a number of occasions, and almost every time he walked me out onto the porch, he would look out theatrically on the city before us—on the Capitol that was sacked but not burned—and say, "Rome hasn't fallen!"

One time, though, he said, "Rome hasn't fallen—yet."

# ABOUT THE AUTHOR

JEFFREY GOLDBERG joined *The Atlantic* in 2007 as a national correspondent and was named the magazine's 15th editor in chief in 2016. He is also the moderator of *Washington Week With The Atlantic* on PBS. In 2022, 2023, and 2024, *The Atlantic* won the National Magazine Award for General Excellence, the highest honor bestowed by the magazine industry. Under Goldberg's leadership, *The Atlantic* has won the first Pulitzer Prizes in its history.

Before joining *The Atlantic*, Goldberg served first as Middle East correspondent, and then as Washington correspondent, for *The New Yorker*. Earlier in his career, he was a writer for *The New York Times Magazine* and *New York* magazine. He began his career as a police reporter for *The Washington Post*. Goldberg is the author of *Prisoners: A Story of Friendship and Terror*. A former fellow of the American Academy in Berlin, he also served as a public-policy scholar at the Woodrow Wilson International Center for Scholars and as the distinguished visiting fellow at the Carnegie Endowment for International Peace. Goldberg is the recipient of numerous awards, including the National Magazine Award for reporting, the Daniel Pearl Award for reporting, the Overseas Press Club award for human-rights reporting, and the International Consortium of Investigative Journalists Prize for best investigative reporting.